MY HAIR IS PROFESSIONAL TOO!

April Maria Williams, Esq.

JumpTime Publishing

JUMPTIME PUBLISHING

The characters and events portrayed in this book are fictitious. Any similarity to real persons, living or dead, is coincidental and not intended by the author.

ISBN-13: 978-1-7378595-0-5

Cover design by: JumpTime Publishing
Printed in the United States of America

This book is dedicated to the only person that knows what my heart sounds like from the inside, My Love Arius.

Table of Contents

Special Acknowledgements

I would like to give a special thanks to my Law School
FAMULY,
Jomayra Belmonte
Ciji Jackson
Sabah Muhammad
for your editorial assistance with this publication.

PREFACE

I decided to wear my hair natural years ago (2007) in my undergraduate studies when wearing your hair natural was not as common as it is today. My hair was not what people would consider, "good hair", so at the time the people around me, including my family, thought I was crazy for wanting to wear my hair natural. Specifically, because I received a bachelor's in business and corporate America was not keen on me wearing my hair as such.

Over the years I have worked in many environments, and I've had many people say many different things about my hair and its texture. I had people ask to touch my hair, as if it was a show, and ask how did you get it to stay so still, or why is your hair so big. But that did not stop me from wanting and continuing to wear my natural hair.

When I was in law school, a professor gave a presentation and it discussed what was considered professional and what was not considered professional. When the presentation discussed hair, many of the styles that were presented in the presentation were ethnic hairstyles, while on the extreme side, those hairstyles were considered unprofessional. I was appalled by the presentation and wanted to do further research to figure out why African American or Black hairstyles were considered unprofessional.

At my law school, you are required to write a legally sound argumentative upper-level paper (25 pages or more) in order to graduate. The paper has to discuss a legal issue, present evidence regarding the issue, laws to support or oppose the legal issue and you have to present a legal resolution to the issue at hand. This paper was written for an independent study for course credit under the direction of Professor Markita D. Cooper, as a part of the upper level curriculum requirement. I took Professor Cooper's employment law course as an elective during my second year of study in law school.

During that course, the major case discussed in this paper, EEOC v. Catastrophe Mgmt. Solutions, released its decision right around the time the class discussed the topic on physical appearance under Title VII in our course book. It was through that discussion I decided to write on the topic of hair styles Akin to African Culture for my upper level requirement. I explained why hairstyles akin to African culture were not considered professional and how the lack of protection, because of the immutable (or unchangeable) texture of African American hair, should be illegal. I coined the paper,
My Hair Is Professional TOO!.

The paper explored the evolution of natural hair and why it's not being considered the norm or professional backed by historical evidence. I gave a detailed analysis of the case laws that have been put in place, that garner no protection to hairstyles akin to African or Black culture. I also explore the perception of African American hair in the workplace and give scientific evidence as to why Black hair should be protected from discrimination. Lastly, I offer a solution as to how we can, without violating other laws, protect Black hair.

This paper was initially submitted to the legal journal, The Southern Journal of Policy and Justice, and was publish in 2019 as a part of their Normalizing Blackness: Assessing the Legal Ramifications of Implicit Bias against the African American Community in the Criminal Justice System, the Workplace and Policy edition. The paper previously was only available through the purchase of Southern Journal of Policy and Justice Journal and on the legal website Westlaw. I decided that as some protective laws have been enacted and more and more Black people are becoming comfortable wearing natural hair styles, the world needed to know how and why Black people are still fighting for equality when it comes to professionalism in the workplace as it relates to hair styles akin to African culture.

Turning this paper into a book makes My Hair Is Professional TOO! available to all who see this issue as a problem and opens the eyes of those who turn a blind eye to the issue. When it comes to natural hair styles, there are no federal statutory laws that prohibited this type of discrimination. However, there is case law that has allowed this discrimination to continue when challenged. As the great Maya Angelou once said, “I have great respect for the past. If you don't know where you've come from, you don't know where you're going....” In order to stop the discrimination, we have to know what laws continue to allow the discrimination.

1 Case laws are based on decisions of courts as opposed to constitutions, statues, regulations. Case Law, CORNELL LAW SCHOOL: LEGAL INFORMATION INSTITUTE, WWW.LAW.CORENLL.EDU, https://www.law.cornell.edu/wex/case_law (last visited July 4, 2020).

Akin to African Culture

The use of the term Akin to African Culture was used to explain the style of hair. The term African does not negate that these styles are just as American as African or Black Americans. The term is used to identify with the ancestral background many African or Black Americans have long since identified with. The terminology should not be dismissed as not being favorable or to be considered any less a part of the African or Black American culture.

My Hair is Professional Too!: A Case Study and Overview of Laws Pertaining to Workplace Grooming Standards and Hairstyles Akin to African Culture

I. Introduction

Imagine being turned down for a job because of the way your hair grows and appears naturally. Imagine having to go through drastic measures to obtain a look to fit into someone else's idea of professionalism. Especially, when you know that your hair and appearance have nothing to do with the quality of your work, your level of education, or your ability to perform the tasks of the job in question. The trade-off is either wearing your hair in its natural state with the styles best suited for your hair texture or wearing hairstyles that employers deem to be appropriate in the workplace. Under the current laws, an employer has the right to refuse to hire, fire, or take other adverse action against African American employees who wear braids,[i] dreadlocks,[ii] or other natural hairstyles.[iii]

I decided to wear my hair in its natural hair texture in 2007, right before I graduated from The University of Toledo with a Master of Arts. I was at a point in my life where I was tired of wearing my hair in a relaxer,[iv] in hair extensions,[v] and in hair weaves. [vi] I was also tired of repeating the same hair cycles. I would get a relaxer, wear my hair straight for a period of time, then my hair would break off, causing the beautician to cut large amounts of my hair off. I would refuse to put a relaxer in my hair for a few months and then start the same cycle all over again that rendered the same results.

Being an Elite Athlete[vii] and having to stay physically fit, maintaining these hairstyles became increasingly difficult. However, my family taught me that wearing my hair straight was appropriate. And through my observations of African American[viii] working women, I learned that straight hairstyles were preferred by employers. Even my college teammates and friends could not understand why I wanted to go from wearing my hair straight—which was well accepted in society—to wearing it in a kinky afro[ix]—which is commonly associated with being rebellious and uncaring as to your appearance.[x] I wanted to embrace my beautiful, natural hair texture and to also stop the pattern of repeated damage to my hair. I was ready to embrace my roots and get my hair back to a healthy state by wearing styles that were akin to African culture and styles that were traditionally worn by people with kinkier hair textures. However, I did not expect to enter into the workplace as an educated woman and hear my supervisor say that my natural hair looked "fun" and was a "little too big" to wear to work. In those moments, I felt my hairstyle was more important to my employer than my level of competency to complete my work-related tasks.

My personal story is not unique.[xi] African American women in the workplace struggle with whether they should wear their natural hair textures or conform to the societal acceptance of straight hairstyles. In a story that made national news in 2015, two African American women (one who worked for a North Carolina news station and the other who was a college sophomore interning at the news station), made a short video showing the one coworker with thick, curly, natural, blonde hair and the other coworker with a short, straight bob haircut.[xii] The woman with the straight bob hair cut explained to the younger woman with the thick, curly hair that if she wanted to be taken seriously on the job, the younger woman would need to straighten her hair as she got older in order to please the people she worked with.[xiii] And while the short video was cute and funny, it really put the spotlight on African American hair, the corporate culture, and the workplace surrounding African American hair.

For another example, consider the story of 21-year-old Charles Craddock. Craddock was hired at a Cedar Point Amusement Park in Ohio (Company) and according to Craddock, he was told prior to moving into the park's dormitory that he had to cut his dreadlocks if he wanted to continue working for the Company.[xiv] Craddock's story was contested by the Company, stating that Craddock's departure was due to his noncompliance with the company's grooming policy prior to moving into the dorms.[xv] However, Craddock recalled wearing dreadlocks during the skype interview and asking if his hair would be an issue. [xvi] The interviewer responded that his dreadlocks would not be an issue as long as he kept them pinned up.[xvii] Ultimately, Craddock refused to cut his hair and as a result, Craddock's employment with the company was terminated.[xviii]

News anchor Brittany Noble of Jackson, Mississippi, was fired after filing a formal workplace discrimination complaint with the EEOC.[xix] Noble is an award-winning journalist who was given the green light by her new director to wear her natural hair.[xx] Only a month after wearing her natural hair, she was pulled into the office and told that her "natural hair [was] unprofessional and the equivalent to throwing on a baseball cap to go to the grocery store." She was told that, "Mississippi viewers needed to see a beauty queen."[xxi] After filing multiple failed complaints with the new station's parent company, she looked to the EEOC for relief.[xxii] Not long after that she was fired [xxiii]

As recent as August of 2020, news anchor Symone Woolridge was targeted by a viewer for wearing her hair in braids on air.[xxiv] The viewer told Woolridge that her hair was unprofessional and that braids were a part of the teenage culture.[xxv] When the news anchor took the comment to social media, she received a number of encouraging comments, likely from other black people who had experienced this type of discrimination.[xxvi] Woolridge commented to the viewer that her management team had approved of her hair style but the viewer was not pleased.[xxvii] If her employer wanted to appease their viewers, Woolridge could have been told to change her hair or even fired, and it would be completely legal.

There are countless stories of discrimination in the workplace for choosing to wear hairstyles akin to African culture. Title VII of the Civil Rights Act of 1964 (Title VII) generally protects against racial discrimination regarding the terms and conditions of employment.[xxviii] However, there are no federal protections afforded to those choosing to wear dreadlocks, nor is there any recourse for choosing to wear braids.[xxix] As interpreted by the courts, Title VII does not prohibit discrimination against African Americans who choose to wear their natural hair textures in hairstyles akin to African culture, such as braids and dreadlocks. Because most workplace-grooming standards are neutral and are applied to all employees, the policies are not actionable by African American employees who face discrimination for wearing hairstyles akin to African culture.[xxx]

Title VII provides the floor for protection.[xxxi] However, a state may provide greater protection under state law, similar to the District of Columbia's Human Rights law, that provides protections against discrimination based on personal appearance.[xxxii] Because the federal law does not provide this protection, states should amend their civil rights statutes to prohibit employment discrimination against African Americans who wear their natural hair textures and hairstyles akin to their culture. While many states have civil rights statutes that protect against discrimination based on race, color, and national origin,[xxxiii] many states do not protect against discrimination based on cultural differences.

This book will focus on workplace-grooming standards that prohibit braids, dreadlocks, two-strand twists,[xxxiv] and other cultural hairstyles worn by African Americans. This book argues that these "neutral" standards discriminate against African American workers because they may be lawfully fired based on an employer's subjective view of what hairstyles are considered professional. This book proposes that states amend their constitutions to include a section that prohibits discrimination based on an employee's physical appearance.

II. Workplace Perceptions of African American Natural Hair and Culturally Based Hairstyles

African American hair has become a hot-button issue with the natural hair movement and the recent court ruling against wearing dreadlocks in the workplace in *EEOC v. Catastrophe Mgmt. Solutions.*[xxxv] There has been a general misconception that wearing hairstyles akin to African culture in the workplace is unprofessional.[xxxvi] Simple google searches reveal that employers and people in general feel that an African American's natural hair and styles akin to African culture are unacceptable in the workplace.[xxxvii] The idea referred to as the "transparency phenomenon" suggests that white people consider their culture to be the norm, ignoring that the perception only considers what is normal in their race.[xxxviii] These norms in turn cross over into the workplace where many African Americans are discriminated against. The view is that hairstyles akin to African culture are unconventional and unfavorable to company perceptions in making them competitive in the industries they serve.[xxxix] As a result, many African American women have resorted to wearing hair weaves, wigs,[xl] relaxers, or straight natural hair to fit into what white culture has determined to be the norm in a professional setting.[xli]

Many African Americans that choose to wear hairstyles that are akin to African culture in a white-dominated American workforce are met with some resistance.[xlii] Even in African American communities, wearing hairstyles such as braids and dreadlocks have been less accepted because African Americans are aware that these styles are just not acceptable in the workplace.[xliii] For example, the President of Hampton University, a Historically Black University (HBCU), banned dreadlocks and cornrows.[xliv] He explained that the prohibition of these hairstyles helped students obtain corporate level positions.[xlv] Also, Ayana Lindsey, a 2016 senior at Spelman College (another HBCU) was told, "when [students are] preparing for job interviews and career fairs, [] professors and career-planning advisers will strongly suggest that girls who normally wear their hair natural opt for straighter hair to appeal to the most conservative of employers."[xlvi]

The problem with the perception of African American hair equating to unprofessional in the workplace is that it negates the job skills or educational training that African Americans have worked hard to obtain.[xlvii] Critics of African Americans wearing hairstyles akin to African culture feel that because these hairstyles are changeable or *mutable*, they are not being discriminatory under the law.[xlviii] It boils down to the culture in America being unwilling to understand the plight of African Americans as it pertains to the tribulations they face when trying to make their natural hair textures fit into societal standards of professionalism.[xlix] Standards that are set and defined by one race.

Therefore, without a sound understanding of the difficulties faced by African Americans as it pertains to wearing hairstyles that are in line with societal standards, African Americans are being consciously and unconsciously discriminated against in the workplace.[l]

Societal perceptions limit opportunities by forcing many African American employees and applicants to choose between acquiring employment, retaining employment, advancing on the job, and wearing hairstyles akin to African culture. The law should not support the forced choice between wearing hairstyles akin to African culture over employment.

III. The History of Conformity to Societal Standards and the New Wave of African Americans Embracing Their Natural Look

Since African Americans received their freedom, they have traditionally strived to fit into the societal standards that have been set.[li] Madam C.J. Walker, while not being the inventor of the relaxer or the hot comb,[lii] aided in supplying products to African American men and women so that they could, on a regular basis, achieve the straight-hair look by using hair straightening tools and chemicals.[liii] Walker created a market for these tools and products for African American hair, which has turned into a money-making industry with projections of the market being worth over $761 million dollars by the end of 2017.[liv] However, the market saw a slowdown in certain areas with more and more African American women deferring from using relaxers and weaves and opting to wear their natural hair.[lv] In 2018, the industry was estimated to be $2.51 billion, more than double previous estimates and projected to be over a trillion dollars by 2021.[lvi]

The 1960s, 1970s, and early 1980s began a back-to-natural movement in the African American hair industry with more women and men wearing their natural afros.[lvii] During these time periods, African Americans were finding a voice in a time where blunt racism against African Americans was prevalent in all aspects of life, including African American hair.[lviii] In the 1970s, Afros were sometimes associated with the false narratives surrounding the Black Panther Party and has since led to natural hair being associated with being radical or a threat to society and societal standards.[lix] By the late 1980s and early 1990s, many African Americans began wearing the Jheri Curl.[lx] The Jheri Curl gave a permanent, softer appearance to the texture of African American hair and was more accepted in society than the natural afro.[lxi]

Later, many African American women and men traded wearing afros and Jheri curls for looks such as relaxed hair, hair weaves, and low haircuts for men.[lxii] In recent years, however, more and more women and men have been foregoing the chemicals and wearing natural hair afros, braids, and dreadlocks. With the growing knowledge of the concerns associated with wearing chemically processed hair and the effects on hair from hair extensions, many African Americans—women in particular—are embracing their natural hair textures, while subtly trying to find ways to fit their natural hair into society and workplace standards of professionalism. Unfortunately, this trend back to natural hair and wearing hairstyles akin to African culture has yet to become fully accepted in the workplace.

IV. Title VII Of The Civil Rights Act Of 1964

Congress enacted Title VII of the Civil Rights Act of 1964 to protect against discrimination in the workplace based on race, color, religion, sex, or national origin.[lxiii] The statute makes it illegal "to limit, segregate, or classify [] employees or applicants for employment in any way which would deprive or tend to deprive any individual of employment opportunities."[lxiv] However, the statute makes no mention of what race is or how it is defined, nor does the statue speak on cultural or biological differences that exist between people of different races.[lxv] Because race was not defined in the statute, courts have relied on dictionary definitions in its analysis to explain the meaning of race. The dictionary definition refers to race as, "[a] characteristic[] distribution of physical characteristics determined by heredity," not necessarily cultural differences.[lxvi] Courts have excluded cultural characteristics from statutory protections, holding that Title VII only covers *immutable* characteristics.[lxvii] Court cases uniformly view hairstyles as a *mutable* characteristic, and therefore excludes braids, dreadlocks, and other hairstyles akin to African culture from antidiscrimination protections. The Equal Employment Opportunity Commission (EEOC), a federal agency that administers and enforces civil rights laws in the workplace, has defined race discrimination to apply to hairstyles akin to African culture, but these findings have been rejected by courts.[lxviii] The EEOC has provided guidance for employers on what is considered discrimination as it applies to a person's dress code.[lxix]

According to the EEOC, an employer may establish a uniform dress code but "if the dress code conflicts with some workers' ethnic beliefs or practices, a dress code must not treat some employees less favorably because of their national origin," as it would be considered discrimination.[lxx] "In general, an employer may establish a dress code which applies to all employees or employees within certain job categories."[lxxi] The exceptions to the dress code comes into play in four instances: (1) when the dress code interferes with the employee's ethnic beliefs or practices; (2) when the dress code interferes with the employee's religious practices and the employee requests an accommodation; (3) where the dress code would cause an undue hardship; or (4) when the employee has a disability that requires an accommodation to the dress code.[lxxii] Courts, however, have been unmoved by the EEOC's claim of protection for African Americans who wear hairstyles akin to African culture because the EEOC has contradicted their own claims of protection.[lxxiii]

The EEOC in the recent *Catastrophe Mgmt. Solutions*[lxxiv] case claimed protections for an African American woman who was denied employment for wearing her hair in dreadlocks, but in a separate EEOC agency hearing, the EEOC failed to find standing for a claim brought by an African American male who was discriminated against for being forced to cut his braids.[lxxv] The EEOC agency decision cited *Willingham v. Macon Tel. Pub. Co.*, which held grooming policies are typically "outside the scope of federal employment discrimination statutes because they do not discriminate on the basis of *immutable* characteristics or certain fundamental rights."[lxxvi] Thus, contradicting its current stance on what hairstyles are discriminatory.[lxxvii]

Because the EEOC has not given a reasonable explanation for its change on the issue of appropriateness of hairstyles akin to African culture, courts are reluctant to agree that employers are prohibited from discriminating against persons who wear hairstyles akin to African culture.[lxxviii] The lack of protection afforded under Title VII and the courts' reluctance to follow the EEOC guidelines shows that there is a strong need for legislation to address the disparity that African Americans face in the workplace when wearing hairstyles akin to African culture.

V. Title VII Case Law and Hairstyles Akin to African Culture

When claims for discrimination based on hairstyles are evaluated by the court system, the *immutable* verses *mutable* standard is employed.[lxxix] *Immutable* refers to characteristics not easily altered such as, "race, color, or natural origin or characteristics more closely associated with a particular ethnic group."[lxxx] *Mutable* refers to characteristics that are within a person's ability to easily alter.[lxxxi] The discussion surrounding hair discrimination has been on the radar of the court system since the enactment of Title VII, which protects against discrimination in the workplace for certain protected classes. Some of the first cases to come before the justice system dealing with hair discrimination involved men who brought claims regarding the length of their hair and sideburns.

In *Fagan v. National Cash Register Co.*, Fagan, a male employee who had been working with the company for several years in their Technical Service Department, brought a sex discrimination claim against his employer for requiring him to conform to a grooming policy that limited the length of his hair.[lxxxii] The court in this case did an in-depth analysis of the reasoning for the enactment of Title VII.[lxxxiii] This analysis found that sex discrimination was a basis for the statute because in the past women were discriminated against solely because they were women.[lxxxiv] The court concluded that this was not the case in *Fagan,* as he was not denied the right to work because of his hair.[lxxxv] The court held:

> Congress sought to establish equal occupational opportunities, an equal right to available employment, equal pay for equal work and equal working conditions. It was not planned for the Act to be used to interfere in the promulgation and enforcement of general rules of employment, deemed essential by the employer, where the direct or indirect economic effect upon the employee was nominal or non-existent . . . [and] never intended to permit an employee to set in motion either federal or state employment machinery merely because he wishes to wear his hair longer than the company rules prescribe.[lxxxvi]

The court also ruled that an employer may not discriminate against an employee as it pertains to an *immutable* characteristic,[lxxxvii] but that a person's "hair length readily can be changed, [and that person] may be required to conform to reasonable grooming standards."[lxxxviii] Lastly, the court concluded that an employer has a right to be viewed favorably by the public and to maintain an image that garners favorable acceptance in the competitive industries they serve.[lxxxix]

Similarly, in *Willingham v. Macon Tel. Publ'g. Co.*, Alan Willingham, a display or copy layout artist claimed that the sole basis for the employer's refusal to hire him was an objection to the length of his hair.[xc] In this case, the plaintiff went on an interview with the defendant employer and was not hired by the employer because of his shoulder length hair.[xci] The plaintiff asserted a Title VII claim for sex discrimination claiming that the defendant's refusal to hire him based on the length of his hair was a violation of Title VII because the same criteria did not apply to women.[xcii] The court reasoned that:

> an employer cannot have one hiring policy for men

> and another for women if the distinction is based on some fundamental right. But a hiring policy that distinguishes on some other ground, such as grooming codes or length of hair, is related more closely to the employer's choice of how to run his business than to equality of employment opportunity.[xciii]

The court held that while it was unlawful under Title VII to discriminate based on sex, in this case, the discrimination was not based on sex but "upon grooming standards" and thus, Title VII did not apply to this case.[xciv] The court also stated:

> hair length is not immutable and . . . [the] employee enjoys no constitutional protection. If the employee objects to the grooming code he has the right to reject it by looking elsewhere for employment, or alternatively he may choose to subordinate his preference by accepting the code along with the job.[xcv]

The court also noted that Title VII was enacted to afford equal opportunity in employment practices and "not to limit an employer's right to exercise his informed judgment as to how best to run his shop."[xcvi]

The logic and reasoning used for finding that hair length is not an *immutable* characteristic has transcended in its application in alleged hair discrimination cases. In *Rogers v. Am. Airlines, Inc.*, an African American employee of American Airlines sought damages for the enactment of a grooming policy that prohibited employees from wearing all-braided hairstyles.[xcvii] American Airlines permitted the employee to wear her hair as she chose when off work but she was required "to pull her hair into a bun and wrap a hairpiece around the bun during working hours."[xcviii] The plaintiff in that case sought relief under the Thirteenth Amendment[xcix] and under Title VII, claiming that the policy discriminated against black women and the "denial of the right to wear her hair in the [cornrows] style intrude[d] upon her rights and discriminate[d] against her."[c] The court in *Rogers* ruled that because the grooming policy applied equally to men and women, black or white, the policy was not discriminatory.[ci] The court distinguished this by explaining that a policy that prohibited an "afro or a bush" would fall under the protections of Title VII as an *immutable* characteristic while others would not.[cii] The court also noted that American Airlines grooming policy was important to "protect a conservative and business-like image, a consideration recognized as a bona fide business purpose." [ciii] The court also analogized *Garcia v. Gloor*, where the court upheld an employer policy that prohibited employees from speaking any language other than English because "Title VII is directed only at specific impermissible bases of discrimination—race, color, religion, sex, or national origin. National origin must not be confused with ethnic or sociocultural traits."[civ] Because the Plaintiff in *Rogers* failed to show that American Airlines engaged in a "practice of creating a working environment heavily charged with ethnic or racial discrimination," the policy was just as "evenhanded" as the no-Spanish-speaking policy in *Garcia*.[cv]

In *Carswell v. Peachford Hosp.*, the plaintiff, an African American female, alleged that she was discriminated against when she was fired because of the style of her hair.[cvi] The plaintiff reported to work with cornrow braids and colored beads on the ends.[cvii] Her supervisor reacted negatively, as the beads made noise when the plaintiff moved.[cviii] The plaintiff was also told by the supervisor that her hairstyle was inappropriate."[cix] The next day, prior to reporting to work, her supervisor called her and told her that she could not wear the hairstyle to work.[cx] The plaintiff argued that "a policy which prohibits the wearing of this hairstyle would have a disparate impact[cxi] on members of the black race."[cxii] The court used the reasoning from *Willingham v. Macon Telegraph Publ'g Co.* and quoted *Garcia*, which held that employers are barred from discriminating only

> on the basis of *immutable* characteristics, such as race and national origin. . . but a hiring policy that distinguishes on some other ground, such as grooming codes or length of hair, is related more closely to the employer's choice of how to run his business than to equality of employment opportunity.[cxiii]

The court also dispelled the disparate impact claims by reasoning that no other employees have been discriminated against for refusing to remove their braids.[cxiv] The court concluded by stating that "an evenhanded application of a reasonable grooming standard does not constitute racial discrimination" when an employee refuses to adhere to the policy.[cxv]

In *McBride v. Lawstaf, Inc.*, the plaintiff asserted that the defendant engaged in a pattern of discrimination by not hiring otherwise qualified candidates that wore braided hairstyles.[cxvi] The court found that the plaintiff "fail[ed] to prove the element of protected activity, as they fail[ed] to show either that [the] defendant's conduct was in violation of Title VII or that her belief as to its discriminatory nature was reasonable."[cxvii] The court in this case offered no real explanation or reasoning as to how they came to this conclusion, except to cite the holding in *Rogers* that braided hairstyles were not protected.[cxviii]

However, in *Hollins v. Atlantic Co.*, Eunice Hollins, an Atlantic Company manufacturing employee, brought a claim against her employer for discrimination under disparate treatment when she was told that she had to receive prior approval before changing her hairstyle.[cxix] The plaintiff was told that prior to changing her hairstyles, she needed to present pictures of the hairstyle for approval by her supervisors.[cxx] On one occasion, the plaintiff arrived at work wearing finger waves;[cxxi] she was told by her supervisor that her hairstyle was unacceptable to the company because it was "too different and did not meet company policy," as being neat and well-groomed to conform to workplace safety concerns.[cxxii] On another occasion, Hollins wore a ponytail to work, the same hairstyle of five white female employees, but was told by her supervisor "that the new style was 'too drastic' and reminded her that she had been instructed to ask about new [hair] styles before changing."[cxxiii] The court noted that the five white women were not required to bring pictures of their hairstyles prior to changing them.[cxxiv] Hollins was subjected to this treatment over the course of her employment with Atlantic Company.[cxxv] The court in this case found that the plaintiff's claim *did* meet the threshold of a disparate treatment claim, because the other women employees were not subjected to the same treatment.[cxxvi] The Court reasoned that the company's argument that Hollin's hairstyles were not actually comparable to other employee's without providing supporting evidence was reason enough to reverse the lower court' ruling.[cxxvii] The case was remanded back to the district court on Hollins's disparate treatment claim.[cxxviii]

Lewis v. UPS is another case where courts have been unwilling to accept hairstyles that are akin to African culture.[cxxix] Lewis, a delivery driver, brought a claim against his employer because his manager threatened to fire him for wearing dreadlocks that bulged outside his cap.[cxxx] The UPS dress code required Lewis to wear a UPS issued cap but was unclear as to how the hair had to fit under the cap.[cxxxi] Lewis claimed he wore his dreadlocks for religious reasons,[cxxxii] however, the employer was unaware of Lewis' religious reasons for wearing dreadlocks and therefore, the threat of being fired was considered innocent under the law.[cxxxiii] Lewis also claimed that because the employer's policy was unclear in regards to the length of the hair and the fact that other employees were not asked to cut their hair, he was being discriminated against.[cxxxiv] However, the court stated:

> the standards for male employee hair . . . must appear businesslike. [The standards] did not address hair issues such as those of [the employee], . . .it is reasonable to assume that the mass of hair beneath such a hat would grow to such a size that most employers would consider it unprofessional in appearance. . . .Vagueness of the policy alone, however, without something more, cannot sustain a claim [of] discrimination.[cxxxv]

Pitts v. Wild Adventures provides another example

of the lack of protection afforded to African Americans in the workplace.[cxxxvi] Patricia Pitts, an employee at the Wild Adventures theme park, was approached by her manager who stated that she disapproved of her cornrows and that she should get her hair done in a "pretty style."[cxxxvii] The employee attempted to comply and later came to work wearing two-strand twists but was told that the hairstyle had the appearance of dreadlocks.[cxxxviii] On another occasion, Pitts refused to change her hairstyle and was "issued a memo that prohibited dreadlocks, cornrows, beads, and styles that are not covered by a hat/visor."[cxxxix] After Pitts' repeated complaints that the policy was discriminatory in nature, her repeated written reprimands, and a denied promotion; Pitts was terminated.[cxl] The court held that the defendant (Wild Adventures) was entitled to summary judgment under Title VII because Pitts failed to file a charge of discrimination with the EEOC within the filing guidelines.[cxli] The court dismissed Pitts' disparate treatment claim citing to *Willingham* and *Rogers*, concluding that "[g]rooming policies are typically outside the scope of federal employment discrimination statutes because they do not discriminate on the basis of *immutable* characteristics."[cxlii] The court stated that "all-braided hairstyle[s] [are] not an *immutable* characteristic. It is an easily changed characteristic, and, even if socioculturally associated with a particular race or nationality, [it] is not an impermissible basis for distinctions in the application of employment practices by an employer."[cxliii] The court concluded, using section 1981 of the Civil Rights Act, which prohibits discrimination based on *immutable* characteristics, that the claim was not valid because "there [was] no evidence that the policy was only enforced against African-Americans."[cxliv] The court stated that, "[d]readlocks and cornrows are not *immutable* characteristics, and an employer policy prohibiting these hairstyles [does] not implicate a fundamental right. The fact that the hairstyle might be predominantly worn by a particular protected group is not sufficient to bring the grooming policy within the scope of [Title VII] prohibitions."[cxlv]

In *Eatman v. UPS*, Eatman, a United Postal Service (UPS) delivery driver filed a claim alleging discrimination for being forced to wear a hat over his dreadlocks.[cxlvi] UPS instituted a grooming policy that mandated that employees with "unconventional" hairstyles, including dreadlocks, braids, cornrows, a dew rag, and a ponytail, had to wear either a hat, a woolen beanie,[cxlvii] a sun-visor, or a mesh or canvas baseball cap while driving the UPS truck.[cxlviii] Eatman initially decided to wear the woolen beanie but found that the hat damaged his hair and decided to forgo wearing the hat despite being told by his supervisor on numerous occasions that he was not conforming to company policy.[cxlix] The court used the reasoning from *Rogers* and *Garcia*, citing that Title VII does not prohibit discrimination on the basis of dreadlocked hair even if the style is socioculturally linked to a particular race or nationality.[cl] The court also dispelled Eatman's disparate impact[cli] claims because he lacked viable statistical evidence that African American workers were disproportionately affected. Eatman's religious claims failed because his "refusal to wear a hat did not stem from a religious aversion to hats . . . [as] neither Protestantism nor Nubianism proscribes hats." Thus, the court did not find in favor of Eatman.[clii]

In *Eatman* and the prior case discussions, courts were unwilling to find that African Americans who wore hairstyles akin to African culture were protected using the same logic in hair length cases, finding that these hairstyles were *mutable* or changeable.

In the most recent case ruling from the Eleventh Circuit, *EEOC v. Catastrophe Mgmt. Solutions*, Chastity Jones' job offer was rescinded with Catastrophe Management Solutions when she refused to cut her dreadlocks.[cliii] The court held that wearing dreadlocks, while being "culturally associated with race," was not an *immutable* characteristic and thus, was not protected under Title VII.[cliv] According to the amended complaint filed by the EEOC, dreadlocks is a common manner of wearing hair that is best suited for the hair texture of African Americans; and even without manipulating the hair to turn it into a dreadlock, the hair texture automatically forms into a coil similar to a dreadlock.[clv] The EEOC further argued that "prohibition of dreadlocks in the workplace constitutes race discrimination because dreadlocks are a manner of wearing the hair that is physiologically and culturally associated with people of African descent."[clvi]

The district court dismissed the claim stating that "a hairstyle . . . closely associated with a particular ethnic group is a *mutable* characteristic."[clvii] The court of appeals stated that the EEOC's attempt to allege disparate treatment[clviii] to assert a disparate impact claim was incorrect, as the two theories are distinct from each other.[clix] The EEOC claimed that the "[d]isparate-treatment law normally permits an employer to implement policies that are not intended to harm members of a protected class, even if their implementation sometimes harms those members, as long as the employer has a legitimate, nondiscriminatory, nonpretextual reason for doing so."[clx] However, the court found that this language "merely explains that disparate treatment liability attaches only when an employer *intentionally* harms members of a protected group. It summarizes the familiar framework courts use to assess disparate treatment claims," not disparate impact claims.[clxi] The court also found that the legal definition of race did not apply to dreadlocks because "[dreadlocks] are not beyond the victim's power to alter. . . ."[clxii]

The cultural differences described by the EEOC need to be addressed because of the difference in hair textures of many African Americans.[clxiii] This stems from African Americans hair naturally coiling up into a dreadlock.[clxiv]

The court in *EEOC v. Catastrophe Mgmt. Solutions* raised a concerning question regarding a ruling that protected African Americans based on their culture and such a ruling's application to Non-African Americans who choose to wear their hair in hairstyles akin to African culture.[clxv] The court asked, "whether culture characteristics or traits associated with one racial group can be absorbed by or transferred to members of a different racial group."[clxvi] The EEOC argued that persons that wore hairstyles akin to African culture, who were not in fact African American, would be able to assert a race-based claim as well, but the court was reluctant to follow this theory.[clxvii]

The court in *Catastrophe Mgmt. Solutions* ultimately acknowledged that "in the last sever[al] decades, there have been some calls for courts to interpret Title VII more expansively by . . . encompassing cultural characteristics associated with race."[clxviii] However, the court declined stating: "races as including culture has not been unanimous."[clxix] "In order for plaintiffs to establish a viable prima facie case in Title VII race discrimination cases involving *mutable* characteristics, courts must employ a broader definition of race that is aligned with earlier courts' definitions as well as contemporary understandings of race."[clxx]

However, the job of addressing the impact that neutral-grooming policies have on African Americans who choose to wear hairstyles akin to African culture in the workplace should not fall solely on the courts but on the legislatures as well.

On the motion for rehearing, the Eleventh Circuit declined to exercise its power to grant a new hearing.[clxxi] In a concurring opinion, the court concluded that there was insufficient evidence to find a Title VII violation.[clxxii] The court reasoned that the EEOC failed to state in their complaint that dreadlocks grow naturally in African American's hair without manipulation.[clxxiii] They found that the policy banning dreadlocks was a race-neutral policy that applied equally to men and women.[clxxiv] The court acknowledged *Price*

Waterhouse, where a woman claimed that she was discriminated against based on her demeanor not being feminine enough."[clxxv] The court in *Price Waterhouse* found that discrimination based on a woman not conforming to the stereotype of a woman, was not protected.[clxxvi] The court reasoned that they were not asked to determine whether Catastrophe Mgmt's "grooming policy is enlightened, or whether it makes sense in our multicultural and evolving society" rather whether the EEOC's Title VII claim had merit.[clxxvii] The Court determined that it did not.[clxxviii]

In the dissenting opinion, Justice Martin directly attacked the majority opinion and its expansion of the requirements for a disparate treatment claim, citing,

> "[the] opinion itself shows us that the notion of an "immutable" racial characteristic is fiction. In an effort to give lower courts an example of "the distinction between immutable and mutable characteristics of race," the panel draws a bright line between dreadlocks and an Afro. The panel actually says that while dreadlocks, a "black hairstyle," is a "mutable choice" and therefore not protected, an Afro, "black hair texture," is an "immutable characteristic" and is therefore protected. This distinction is nonsense. If an immutable trait is something that is "beyond the [plaintiff]'s power to alter," then neither dreadlocks nor Afros are immutable traits of black people. Like any hair style, both can be altered."[clxxix]

Justice Martin explained that the court basically eliminated the immutable criteria which would allow discrimination, because it is always in a person's power to change their hairstyles. Without the protection an employer could discriminate against an employee for a trait that should be protected.

Justice Martin further stated,

> "the antidiscrimination principle [is] embodied in Title VII just as much as the discriminatory animus motivating a ban on Afros. Both are distinctly African American racial traits. So, when an employer refuses to hire or promote a black employee on the basis of one of those traits, there is a strong indication that the employee's race motivated the decision."[clxxx]

What Justice Martin articulated is that when an employer does not hire you because of a physical feature that is closely associated with your race, you are being discriminated against because of your race.[clxxxi] In essence, the majority was giving the green light to discriminate based on race which is what disparate treatment claims under Title VII are supposed to protect against.

Justice Martin went on to analyze the case as to how she felt the court should have ruled on the Motion to Dismiss. She used the same case, *Price Waterhouse,* to cite that just as the woman in that case was discriminated against based on how her employer felt a women should look, the same was the case for the EEOC's case where Ms. Jones was not hired based on what Catastrophe Management felt a black person's hair should look like to be deemed professional in a work setting.[clxxxii] Further, using their own race neutral grooming policy to show that by pointing out a race specific stereotype ("*Dreadlocks tend to get messy*"), they were in fact making a "racial preference for employees with characteristically white traits."[clxxxiii] Even though the concurring opinion said *Willingham's* immutable trait criteria did not apply, Justice Martin still felt that the court came to the wrong conclusion because the complaint does allege that dreadlocks "are an immutable trait that satisfies the *Willingham* requirement" and that they are beyond the plaintiff's power to alter."[clxxxiv] In essence the concurring opinion defined the definition of immutable trait to mean naturally occurring but still ruled that the complaint did not alleged that dreadlocks are immutable in striking it down.[clxxxv] Justice Martin concluded that the majority used "Pseudoscience" in drawing their conclusion.[clxxxvi] This case was petitioned to the Supreme Court of the United States, but the court declined to proceed with reviewing the case.[clxxxvii]

These cases illustrate how Title VII provides no protections for African American employees who wear dreadlocks, braids, and other hairstyles closely associated with African culture. In most cases, courts have found that these hairstyles are not *immutable*, ignoring the distinct differences in the hair textures among African Americans and Non-African Americans. The judicial holdings have been unfavorable to individuals who file claims of discrimination for wearing hairstyles that are akin to African culture, finding these styles to be *mutable*.

Courts have, however, held that employers may not discriminate against African Americans that wear their hair in an "unaltered or unmanipulated" afro style.[clxxxviii] In 1976, an African American woman in *Jenkins v. Blue Cross Mut. Hosp. Ins. Inc.*, brought a claim against her employer for racial discrimination after the woman began to wear her afro to work.[clxxxix] The comments made by the employer regarding the African American woman's hair as not being a style representative of the company, coupled with the negative treatment toward the woman by the employer, led the court to conclude that there was racial discrimination present that could be protected under Title VII.[cxc] Thus, one could conclude from *Jenkins* that African Americans wearing their hair in an afro hairstyle would be protected under Title VII.[cxci]

The issue of wearing hairstyles akin to African culture, however, still remains an issue of concern and needs to be addressed to prohibit this type of discrimination in the workplace. Legislative action that prohibits discrimination based on a person's appearance would address the court's concern of *immutability* in *Catastrophe Mgmt. Solutions*, while also addressing the disparate impact that falls on African Americans who wear these hairstyles.[cxcii]

VI. History and Health Concerns for African American Hair

A. Historical Prospective

Prior to the Transatlantic Slave Trade,[cxciii] African hairstyles would indicate a person's family background, tribe, and social status, and "just about everything about a person's identity could be learned by looking at [their] hair."[cxciv] However, during the Transatlantic Slave Trade, African American's natural hair was viewed in a negative light. When Africans were transported over on ships, they were in bondage. Because of this, "their hair became matted with blood, feces, urine, sweat, tears, and dirt [and] upon observing them, some slaves traders referred to [the] slaves' hair as dreadful."[cxcv] This later coined the term *dreadlock* to refer to the coily formation that developed in slaves' hair during the trip to America.[cxcvi] An estimated 11,640,000 Africans were taken from the continent of Africa due to the Transatlantic Slave Trade and with them they brought their hairstyling techniques, such as specially-designed hair combs.[cxcvii]

Cultural distinctions between African American hair began during slavery, when the slaves were given their work assignments. [cxcviii] Slaves that worked in the fields wore their hair in styles similar to their culture, while slaves working in close relations to the white owners "styled their hair in an imitation of their white owners."[cxcix] When slavery was abolished, many African Americans felt the need to fit into society by smoothening their hair texture.[cc] African Americans went to extreme measures to make their hair fit societal standards such as using "a hot chemical mixture that would almost burn their scalp, so [that] they could comb it back and make it look more European and silky."[cci] Throughout the years of hairstyle transitions of African Americans, the need to fit in has taken precedent. Fitting in, however, does not take into account the biological differences and medical concerns that African Americans face when they alter their hair textures to conform to professional workplace standards. Workplace standards set by one race.

B. Biological Differences Between African Americans and Non-African American Hair Textures

In order to understand why there is a need for legislation that addresses the discriminatory impact that neutral-grooming policies have on African Americans, we must note that there are distinguishing biological difference in the hair textures of African Americans and Non-African Americans. Some people believe that race is a social phenomenon created within society, "not genetically distinct branches of humankind," because the differences we commonly associate with race are not supported by any biological evidence.[ccii] However, while all humans have a common biological make up, there are distinct differences as it relates to the genetic make-up of humans among different racial groups.[cciii]

The distinguishing difference in African American and Non-African American hair is in the texture itself. African American hair texture is thicker, drier to the touch than other hair textures, extremely difficult to over-condition, and very fragile.[cciv] The difference is due to the biological distinctions in the size and shape of the hair follicles of African American hair.[ccv] African American hair also tends to produce more oils than Non-African American hair, but due to the tight curls, the oils do not spread evenly, thus causing dryness in African American hair textures.[ccvi] Also, the hair tends to have tight coils and spirals.[ccvii] Further, tightly spiraled hair textures are difficult to brush and comb because it tends to be more dense than other types of hair textures.[ccviii]

These distinct biological differences in the hair textures of African Americans have not been acknowledged by the courts in their decisions regarding employees who wear hairstyles akin to African culture.[ccix] However, because a traditional definition of race is being used and there are no protections under federal law for African Americans that wear hairstyles akin to African culture, the only option African Americans have left is the reliance on the biological differences to show that the use of cultural hairstyles is necessary for many African American hair textures.

C. Potential Dangers of Wearing Relaxers, Weaves, and Heated Hairstyles

For African American women who wear straight hair or hair weaves, there can be health dangers associated with altering their hair textures or wearing straight hair styles. Straightening natural African American hair can be a daunting task, as extreme heat or a relaxer[ccx] is needed to achieve the straight-hair look. Extreme heat (no matter what texture of hair) can cause damage to hair follicles, but because straightening African American hair can severely alter the hair texture, the effects can be more detrimental to African American hair textures.[ccxi] Wearing hair weaves[ccxii] can also have damaging effects on African American hair. Hair weaves can lead to traction alopecia[ccxiii] because of the tugging and pulling on the hair from the scalp that occurs when hair weaves are installed and worn over a period of time.[ccxiv] When choosing the type of hair to be installed as a hair weave, African American women have to consider the effects of using synthetic hair,[ccxv] which burns easily and can mesh with a person's natural hair as opposed to human hair,[ccxvi] which is more resistant to heat but carries a heavier cost.[ccxvii] These risks are minimized when African American women wear their natural hair and hairstyles akin to African culture.

Relaxers have also been found to cause "hair breakage, hair thinning, lack of hair growth, scalp irritation, scalp damage, and hair loss."[ccxviii] While relaxers produce a silky texture of hair, "excessive use of hair [relaxers] is also a cause of widespread hair loss, called scarring alopecia."[ccxix] Because of the chemicals in relaxers,[ccxx] one study has found that excessive use of relaxers has raised the concern that its use leads to uterine leiomyomata or uterine fibroids.[ccxxi] While this study is not conclusive, it is imaginable that when these chemicals enter the blood stream (because they tend to burn the scalp) of its user, there can be detrimental effects.[ccxxii]

African American women who wear relaxers, weaves,

and heated hairstyles are also less likely to exercise on a regular basis for fear of their hair being out of place after paying hundreds of dollars for their hairstyle.[ccxxiii] "Researchers found about two [out of] every five African-American women said they avoid exercise because of concerns about their hair, and researchers say that this is concerning given the United States' obesity epidemic."[ccxxiv] African American women who forego working out to ensure that their hair is presentable in the workplace also raises the same concerns posed by men shaving every day.

Because courts have not considered the specific health concerns related to African American natural hair, specific legislation is necessary to address this problem. The law should not allow an employer to discriminate against African American women who choose not to wear their hair in styles that have traditionally been deemed appropriate in the workplace in light of the health concerns that many of these women face or will face in wearing styles more accepting by society. Style standards that have been set by one race. While most of the health concerns have a greater impact on African American women, it must be acknowledged that African American men have the same hair textures as African American women. When men choose to wear hairstyles akin to African culture, they too are choosing styles that work best for their texture of hair and should not face discrimination for wearing these styles.

D. Courts Willingness to Find a Healthcare Exception for Pseudofollicultitis Barbae (PFB)

Courts have been willing to find a healthcare exception for discriminatory claims brought by African American men who wear beards, finding that health concerns may trump an employer's grooming policy.[ccxxv] Studies have shown that African American men are more prone to develop pseudofolliculitis barbae (PFB),[ccxxvi] commonly referred to as razor bumps, when African American men shave with a razor on a regular basis.[ccxxvii] There is no known cure for PFB, as it only occurs when men shave too closely or too often.[ccxxviii] However, there are dermatologist approved medicines and techniques, such as the use of prescription creams, that African American men can use to treat the bumps and inflammation caused by shaving.[ccxxix]

In *Bradley v. Pizzaco*, a dominos delivery driver, was fired for failing to comply with the franchise owner's no-beard policy. [ccxxx] The plaintiff contended that the no-beard policy violated Title VII because "the no-beard policy deprived him and other African American males suffering from PFB of equal employment opportunities."[ccxxxi] The court held that the employer's business justification of "[it is] common sense that the better our people look, the better our sales will be," was largely speculative and conclusory.[ccxxxii] The case was remanded and the court ordered an "injunction . . . carefully tailored to place Domino's under the minimal burden of recognizing a limited exception to its no-beard policy for African American males who suffer from PFB."[ccxxxiii] The court also found that the customer survey, where only 20% of customers viewed beards unfavorably, was not enough evidence to justify the no-beard policy as a business necessity.[ccxxxiv]

Similarly, in *EEOC v. Trailways, Inc.*, the court found that there was a Title VII claim against the employer's grooming policy because of the extensive research that showed PFB was a condition that affected African American males more so than other races.[ccxxxv] The court in *Trailways* held that while an employer can have a no-beard policy, a person that presents a PFB medical certificate should be provided with an accommodation and failure to provide an accommodation could result in a disparate impact on the African American employees within the company.[ccxxxvi]

The courts' decisions regularly find exceptions to the rule for men with PFB and no-beard policies. Thus, the same logic used in PFB cases can serve as grounds for acknowledging the medical concerns that affect African Americans, women in particular, when it comes to conforming to grooming policies in the workplace and societal standards of professionalism.

If courts are willing to acknowledge that men who shave often stand the risk of developing PFB, courts should be willing to find a health exception for African Americans who wear hairstyles akin to African culture because they have to resort to extreme measures to conform to neutral-grooming policies. Grooming policies set by a standard that only considers one race. Similarly, if courts are made aware of the fact that African

American women are facing medical concerns in order to fit into the societal standards of what is deemed professional, courts should again apply the same standards that are applied in PFB cases. Knowing that PFB affects African American men more so than Non-African American men, there is also a strong argument for men and women who choose to wear hairstyles akin to African culture.[ccxxxvii]

VII. A Legislative Solution: The District of Columbia Provides Protections Based on Personal Appearance to Combat Discrimination

The District of Columbia (D.C.) has enacted a specific discrimination statute known as The D.C. Human Rights Law, that among the many components, protects employees from discrimination based on race, color, genetic information, and personal appearance, including hairstyles.[ccxxxviii] The purpose of the statute is "to secure an end in the District of Columbia to discrimination for any reason other than that of individual merit, including, but not limited to, the enumerated classes."[ccxxxix] The D.C. Human Rights Law was "intended to go above and beyond the protections afforded to employees by Title VII."[ccxl] The personal appearance section of this code is particularly important as it includes hair. The statute's definition of personal appearance includes:

> outward appearance of any person, irrespective of sex, with regard to bodily condition or characteristics, manner or style of dress, and manner or style of personal grooming, including, but not limited to, hair style and beards. It shall not relate, however, to the requirement of cleanliness, uniforms, or prescribed standards, when uniformly applied for admittance to a public accommodation, or when uniformly applied to a class of employees for a reasonable business purpose; or when such bodily conditions or characteristics, style or manner of dress or personal grooming presents a danger to the health, welfare or safety of any individual.[ccxli]

This particular portion of the statue is *important*, as it has the potential to protect African American employees who wear dreadlocks, twists, braids, and other hairstyles akin to African culture from workplace discrimination based on neutral-grooming policies.

Under the D.C. Code, in order to prove a prima facie case of wrongful termination for discrimination, the employee must show:

> (1) she is a member of a protected class; (2) she suffered an adverse employment action; and (3) the unfavorable action gives rise to an inference of discrimination . . . by demonstrating that [the plaintiff] was treated differently from similarly situated employees who are not part of the protected class or by showing that the discharge was not attributable to the two [] common legitimate reasons for discharge. . . . If the plaintiff is able to establish her prima facie case by a preponderance of the evidence, the burden of production switches to the employer to articulate a legitimate, nondiscriminatory reason for its actions.[ccxlii]

This code requires employers to look past an applicant or employee's appearance and to their actual qualifications.[ccxliii] Under this code, the employer must show that a grooming policy that prohibits an employee from wearing hairstyles that are akin to African culture is essential to the job functions and that the reasons for firing or not hiring an employee were legitimate.[ccxliv]

D.C. has a sizeable demographic of African Americans so it makes sense for such a code to be enacted there.[ccxlv] However, D.C.'s large African American population should not be an excuse for other cities and states to not enact such legislation.[ccxlvi] Prior to this legislation, D.C. was not immune to discrimination based on African Americans wearing hairstyles akin to African culture.

In 1987, an African American employee who was employed by Marriott Hotel (Marriott) was threatened and eventually fired for wearing her hair in cornrows.[ccxlvii] Marriott's grooming policy "sought to prohibit extreme faddish hairdos."[ccxlviii] The employee in this case filed a claim with the EEOC, requesting an injunction to prohibit Marriot from firing her.[ccxlix] However, the case was settled after the court of appeals ruled in favor of the employee proceeding with her claim.[ccl] The court found "probable cause to believe Marriott's policy constituted discrimination on the basis of race and personal appearance."[ccli]

Another D.C. case in 1988 involved the Hyatt Hotel (Hyatt), who also had a policy prohibiting the cornrow hairstyle.[cclii] The Hyatt claimed the style was against the "extreme or unusual" section in the grooming policy.[ccliii] This case gained national attention, leading to a boycott of Hyatt hotels and to the EEOC finding that the policy violated Title VII, as it was found to be racially discriminatory.[ccliv] However, the D.C. Office of Human Rights decided not to pursue an investigation of discrimination against Hyatt.[cclv] The plaintiff in this case filed suit in D.C. but was awarded a pre-jury settlement similar to the Marriott case.[cclvi]

The D.C. Human Rights Law could have prevented claims like those mentioned above and can be a framework for legislatures across the country and to our general legislative body. Using this framework, courts will not have to solely focus on whether hairstyles are *immutable* or *mutable*. Instead, this framework provides an alternative analysis that requires an employer to look past a person's physical appearance.

VIII. The Proposal: All Stated Should Enact Legislation to Prohibit Discrimination Based on Physical Appearance Including Hairstyles Akin to African Culture

States have the discretion and ability to provide more protection than what is required by federal law, which would enable all states to adopt additional protections.[cclvii]Accordingly, each state legislature has the power to include a section that provides protection based on a person's physical appearance. Currently, all states have some form of a civil rights statue that protects against discrimination. Adding a law to every state that provides protections for a person's physical appearance, including African Americans who wear their hair in styles akin to African culture is needed.

An appearance statute would also address other forms of discrimination that people of all races face because of their physical appearance. This proposed legislation, like the D.C. Human Rights Law, should apply to all employers regardless of whether they are state or privately owned, no matter how many employees an employer has.[cclviii] The proposed legislation should extend to anyone who is employed by an employer or seeking employment from an employer.[cclix]

Using the D.C. framework, employers will be prohibited from discriminating "against employees based on their outward appearance in recruiting, hiring or promotion. Outward appearance refers to an individual's bodily condition or characteristics, manner or style of dress, and manner or style of personal grooming (hairstyle, beards, etc.)."[cclx] Employers would be required to provide a reasonable accommodation to "allow employees to wear clothing or hairstyles in a style symbolic of race, heritage, or religion, unless there is a reasonable business purpose to prohibit an employee from doing so."[cclxi] A statute that provides these type of protections would specifically address the concerns that many African Americans currently face.[cclxii] When it comes to the appropriateness of hairstyles akin to African culture, as long as the employee maintains "a certain level of cleanliness, wear[s] uniforms, or [meets] other specific standards" deemed to be reasonably related to employment, African American employees would be protected.[cclxiii]

Employers will still be able to retain their prerogative to have reasonable workplace grooming polices to further an employer's business objective, such as business-like appearances, conformity, and unity in look for employees.[cclxiv] Enacting a personal appearance statute will ensure that African Americans are protected in the workplace, while wearing their natural hair textures and hairstyles that many African American workers find more befitting for their hair textures.

IX. Some States Have Taken Steps to Address Hair Discrimination in the Workplace

In June of 2019, California became the first state to ban discrimination in the workplace based on natural hair styles.[cclxv] In a study conducted in conjunction with Dove[cclxvi], National Urban League[cclxvii], Color of Change[cclxviii] and Western Center of Law & Poverty[cclxix], it was revealed that a "black women's hair is 3.4 times more likely to be perceived as unprofessional."[cclxx] The Study also revealed that black women are 80% more likely to change their hair from its natural state to fit in at work.[cclxxi] Since California's bill passage, seven other states including, Washington, Colorado, Virginia, Maryland, New Jersey and New York have all signed into law such bills.[cclxxii] On August 11, 2020, similar legislation was passed by the Nebraska legislatures.[cclxxiii] However, only days later the Governor, Pete Ricketts vetoed the bill, derailing its enactment.[cclxxiv] The Crown Coalition has made incredible headways but without all states having such a law, many African American men and women will continue to face discrimination for wearing styles akin to African culture.

X. Conclusion

African Americans have made undeniable advances since 1865, the year African Americans gained their freedom from slavery. While African Americans are continuing to advance in the workplace, many of them face discrimination for wearing the hairstyles that they believe are best suited for their hair textures. Hairstyles that are akin to African culture are deeply rooted in African American communities and have been worn since the inception of this country. When Title VII was enacted, cultural differences between African Americans and Non-African Americans was not of consideration. As we hopefully move forward toward a more inclusive society, we must look at the disparity faced by individual groups in our society as important if we truly want to continue to "Make America Great."[cclxxv]

With a statute in place to protect against discrimination based on a person's appearance, African American employees will no longer struggle with being employed or wearing natural hairstyles and taking care of their health. Individuals like the African American intern working for the North Carolina news station will not have to worry about being taken seriously on the job because of her decision to wear her hair in styles akin to African culture. And, people like Charles Craddock will not have to choose between wearing their hair in dreadlocks and pursuing employment opportunities. HBCU school leaders will no longer have to ban or discourage their students from wearing hairstyles akin to African Culture. Your hair style choice will no longer be another avenue for race discrimination.

Few states have taken steps toward alleviating this issue and have gained praise for their efforts, but we are hardly at the end of this battle. All states legislatures should enact legislation to prohibit discrimination when wearing hairstyles akin to African culture.

After all, these hairstyles are Professional TOO!

Foot Notes and Comments

The footnotes are written in accordance with the legal formatting from the 20th edition of the Bluebook.

[i]

Braids: taking three or four strains, interweaving them together tightly or loosely to form a braid. merrian-webster.com, https://www.merriam-webster.com/dictionary/braids (last visited Feb. 23, 2017).

[ii] "Dreadlocks, sometimes referred to as dreads or locks, are basically matted ropes of hair that will form naturally if you neglect them. However, they can also be formed on purpose through various methods that allow you to control their shape and make them very attractive. There are several methods that can be used to achieve," the dreadlock hair style. *What Are Dreadlocks?,* howtogetdreads, http://howtogetdreads.com/dreadlock-tutorials/preparing-for-dreadlocks/what-are-dreadlocks/.

[iii] Full discussion later on existing case law regarding discrimination against hairstyles akin to African culture and what hair style is protected. Current laws permit discrimination based on hair style, not taking into account the biological and cultural differences in hair textures. *See* EEOC v. Catastrophe Mgmt. Solutions, 852 F.3d 1018 (11th Cir. 2016.

[iv] A Relaxer or perm "is a lotion or cream that makes hair easy to straighten and manage." It "reduces the curl by altering the chemical structure of the hair, making the hair resistant to returning to its original curly/textured state. . . . usually offer[ing] a straightened result for 6-8 weeks." *What Relaxers Really Do To Your Hair,* BlackDoctor.org, http://blackdoctor.org/216545/what-relaxers-really-do-to-your-hair__trashed/2/.

[v] Hair Extensions: "hair extension method refers to synthetic or human hair being attached to the natural hair of a person with an adhesive, clip-ons, micro links or tape to lengthen the hair an add fullness. Hair extensions are applied strand by strand to the natural hair. It is a very time-consuming method as around 100-300 extensions are added to one person to make the hair look natural. This application of hair is considered the most expensive due to the labor and time it consumes." *Weaves vs Extensions,* Black Hair Media, http://blackhairmedia.com/weave-and-extension/weaves-vs-extensions-2/.

[vi] Hair weave: "synthetic or human hair used to change the appearance of someone's hair by adding hair to their natural hair. Specifically, a weave refers to a style when someone's entire hair is braided. Once the braids are made, a needle is used to sew extensions of hair into the braids. The extensions are sewn from one ear to another. The weave lasts for 6 to 8 weeks." *Weaves vs Extensions,* Black Hair Media, http://blackhairmedia.com/weave-and-extension/weaves-vs-extensions-2/.

[vii] I competed in the sport of Track and Field in college and for four years post-graduation. As an Elite Athlete, I competed in the 2008 Olympic Trials in the Triple Jump. I trained for competitions on average 20-25 hours a week, which had an effect on my hair.

[viii] Many Black American today either identify themselves as African American or Black to be encompassing of the diversity within their ancestral background. The term African American gained its prominence in use during the late 1980's and early 1990's. Thus, the use of the term African and Black culture extends to many groups of people. For further discussion, *see* Isabel Wilkerson, *'African-American' Favored By Many of America's Blacks,* NY Times (1989), https://www.nytimes.com/1989/01/31/us/african-american-favored-by-many-of-america-s-blacks.html (showing that the term "African American" was changed from just black); *see* Shahida Muhammad, *I'm Not African American...I'm Black,* Ebony (June 13, 2012), http://www.ebony.com/news-views/im-not-african-american-im-black (showing that the term "African American" has been used to be politically correct and has a limiting context); *See infra*: Since slavery, it has been thought that persons of a darker skin

and with African features, including hair texture, only encompassed those of African descent. However, the term Black American has been commonly used to encompass both those who identify as Black and those of African descent. *Indivisible, African- Native American Lives in the Americas,* SMITHSONIAN, *http://www.nmai.si.edu/exhibitions/indivisible/index.html (showing the coming together of African and Native Americans); Black Indians An American Story,* RICH-HEMP FILMS, *https://www.richheape.com/black-indians-american-story.htm (showing intermingling of African and Native Americans); see* Dania Santana, *What Is An Afro-Latina? #AmericanLatinos,* EMBRACING DIVERSITY, http://embracingdiversity.us/what-is-an-afro-latina-black-latina/ (defining an Afro Latina as a person who has Black person who comes from Latin America or a person of African descent whose origin is from Latin America); *See* James Mooney, *Myths of the Cherokee, Nineteenth Annual Report, Bureau of American Ethnology, 1897-98* 233 (2015) (stating that as early as the late nineteenth century of the Nineteenth Annual Report of the Bureau of American Ethnology noted that a considerable proportion of the blood of the southern Negro [of the U.S.] is "unquestionably Indian")

[ix] Afro: a hairstyle of tight curls in a full evenly rounded shape. Merriam-Webster.com, https://www.merriam-webster.com/dictionary/Afro (last visited Mar. 2, 2017); Kinky Puff: wearing your natural kinky or curly hair in a ponytail at the top or center of your head. *See* Enell B. Stewart, *7 Cute Summer Puff Styles for Short, Medium and Long Natural Hair,* kinkycurlycoilyme.com (July 11, 2014 at 9:32 AM), https://www.kinkycurlycoilyme.com/7-cute-summer-puff-styles-for-short-medium-and-long-natural-hair/.

[x] Rumeana Jahangir, *How Does Black Hair Reflect Black History?,* BBC News (May 31, 2015), http://www.bbc.com/news/uk-england-merseyside-31438273.

[xi] One of my good friends Lindsay, a Realtor, also decided to wear her hair natural. One of her colleagues asked her if she was going to straighten her hair for a consultation, she had with high end customers. Lindsay found her colleagues question disturbing because she has always appeared professional in dress and in style. Her colleague told her that she didn't even think about what she had said, nor did she realize how offensive her statement was. Lindsay, a top producer in her real estate market area, was being told that if she wanted to get to the next level in her career, she would have to alter her natural appearance in order to gain higher end clients. Lindsay had been in the real estate business for over three years and had seen substantial growth in her business and was currently in the top ten percent of production in the city and surrounding area where she lived and worked. Lindsay was appalled. Wearing her hair in its natural textures and styles akin to African culture had nothing to do with her ability to provide solid real estate services to her clients. While Title VII does not protect independent contractors, the company that Lindsay works for could refuse to allow her to be apart of their company because of her hair style choice. Telephone interview Lindsay Thompson, Realtor, Keller Williams Town and Country (Feb. 6, 2017); *Coverage,* U.S. Equal Employment Opportunity Commission, www.eeoc.gov , https://www.eeoc.gov/employers/coverage-0 (last visited August 30, 2020).

[xii] Hair Bobs: cutting hair into a collarbone, chin-length or cropped hairstyle. *70 Winning Looks With Bob Haircuts for Fine Hair,* The Right Hairstyle (Sep. 3, 2018), http://therighthairstyles.com/5-winning-looks-with-bob-haircuts-for-fine-hair/.; Sheryl Estrada, *Natural Hair: To Straighten or Not To Straighten,* Diversity Inc. (Sept. 22, 2015), http://www.diversityinc.com/news/natural-hair-to-straighten-or-not-to-straighten/.

[xiii] Sheryl Estrada, *Natural Hair: To Straighten or Not To Straighten,* Diversity Inc. (Sept. 22, 2015), http://www.diversityinc.com/news/natural-hair-to-straighten-or-not-to-straighten/.

[xiv] Lee Moran, *Ohio Man, 20, Claims Dreadlocks Cost Him Summer Job at Amusement Park,* Daily News (May 11, 2015, 5:11 AM), www.nydailynews.com, http://www.nydailynews.com/news/national/ohio-man-20-claims-dreadlocks-cost-summer-job-article-1.2217641. Employers can in most instances refuse to hire or even fire employees if they do not approve of an employee wearing hair styles akin to African American culture such as dreadlocks and braids; this adverse employment action would be completely legal under the current Title VII protections. Refer to discuss later how courts have failed to provide protections in these instances under Title VII. *See e.g,.* EEOC v. Catastrophe Mgmt. Solutions, 852 F.3d 1018 (11th Cir. 2016).

[xv] Susanna Kim, *Ohio Man Claims Employer Told Him to Cut His Dreadlocks or Lose Job*, abcnews (May 8, 2015, 5:22 AM), http://abcnews.go.com/Business/ohio-man-claims-employer-told-cut-dreadlocks-lose/story?id=30906401.

[xvi] Lee Moran, *Ohio Man, 20, Claims Dreadlocks Cost Him Summer Job at Amusement Park*, Daily News (May 11, 2015, 5:11 AM), www.nydailynews.com, http://www.nydailynews.com/news/national/ohio-man-20-claims-dreadlocks-cost-summer-job-article-1.2217641.

[xvii] Lee Moran, *Ohio Man, 20, Claims Dreadlocks Cost Him Summer Job at Amusement Park*, Daily News (May 11, 2015, 5:11 AM), www.nydailynews.com, http://www.nydailynews.com/news/national/ohio-man-20-claims-dreadlocks-cost-summer-job-article-1.2217641.

[xviii] Lee Moran, *Ohio Man, 20, Claims Dreadlocks Cost Him Summer Job at Amusement Park*, Daily News (May 11, 2015, 5:11 AM), www.nydailynews.com, http://www.nydailynews.com/news/national/ohio-man-20-claims-dreadlocks-cost-summer-job-article-1.2217641.

[xix] Christina Santi, *Black News Anchor Fired After Wearing "Unprofessional Natural Hair*, EBONY (Jan. 16, 2019), https://www.ebony.com/culture/black-news-anchor-fired-unprofessional-natural-hair/.

[xx] Christina Santi, *Black News Anchor Fired After Wearing "Unprofessional Natural Hair*, EBONY (Jan. 16, 2019), https://www.ebony.com/culture/black-news-anchor-fired-unprofessional-natural-hair/.

[xxi] Christina Santi, *Black News Anchor Fired After Wearing "Unprofessional Natural Hair*, EBONY (Jan. 16, 2019), https://www.ebony.com/culture/black-news-anchor-fired-unprofessional-natural-hair/.

[xxii] Christina Santi, *Black News Anchor Fired After Wearing "Unprofessional Natural Hair*, EBONY (Jan. 16, 2019), https://www.ebony.com/culture/black-news-anchor-fired-unprofessional-natural-hair/.

[xxiii] Christina Santi, *Black News Anchor Fired After Wearing "Unprofessional Natural Hair*, EBONY (Jan. 16, 2019), https://www.ebony.com/culture/black-news-anchor-fired-unprofessional-natural-hair/.

[xxiv] *News Anchor Symone Woolridge Called "Unprofessional" And Childish For Wearing Braids On Air*, emilycottontop.com, https://emilycottontop.com/news-anchor-symone-woolridge-called-unprofessional-and-childish-for-wearing-braids-on-air/ (last visited Aug. 15, 2020).

[xxv] *News Anchor Symone Woolridge Called "Unprofessional" And Childish For Wearing Braids On Air*, emilycottontop.com, https://emilycottontop.com/news-anchor-symone-woolridge-called-unprofessional-and-childish-for-wearing-braids-on-air/ (last visited Aug. 15, 2020).

[xxvi] *News Anchor Symone Woolridge Called "Unprofessional" And Childish For Wearing Braids On Air*, emilycottontop.com, https://emilycottontop.com/news-anchor-symone-woolridge-called-unprofessional-and-childish-for-wearing-braids-on-air/ (last visited Aug. 15, 2020).

[xxvii] *News Anchor Symone Woolridge Called "Unprofessional" And Childish For Wearing Braids On Air*, emilycottontop.com, https://emilycottontop.com/news-anchor-symone-woolridge-called-unprofessional-and-childish-for-wearing-braids-on-air/ (last visited Aug. 15, 2020).

[xxviii] 42 U.S.C. §2000e-2.

[xxix] Sheryl Estrada, *Natural Hair: To Straighten or Not To Straighten*, Diversity Inc. (Sept. 22, 2015), http://www.diversityinc.com/news/natural-hair-to-straighten-or-not-to-straighten/.

[xxx] Discrimination: Race, National Origin, Gender, Religion and Age, §2.21 (Empl. L. 19944).

[xxxi] Florida Lime & Avocado Growers, Inc. v. Paul, 373 U.S. 141, 178 (U.S. 1963).

[xxxii] D.C. Code § 2-1401.01(Enacted Jul. 1 2016); D.C. Code § 2-1401.02; D.C. Code § 2-1401.11.

[xxxiii] State Civil Rights Law, Find Law, findlaw.com, https://statelaws.findlaw.com/civil-rights-laws.html (last visited Sept. 9, 2020).

[xxxiv] Two strand twists: taking small or big parts of the natural hair, twisting them into small sections of hair using [a hair crème or hair dress formula] from roots to tips and throughout the entire head. *How To Create The Perfect Two-Strand Twist Out*, essence (Jul. 12, 2016), http://www.essence.com/2016/07/11/perfect-two-strand-twist-out-how-to.

[xxxv] Alex Janin, *What the Perception of 'Professional' Hair Means for Black Job Seekers*, Take part, (Apr. 13, 2016), http://www.takepart.com/article/2016/04/13/what-perception-professional-hair-means-black-job-seekers; *see generally* EEOC v. Catastrophe Mgmt. Solutions, 852 F.3d 1018 (11th Cir. 2016).To be discussed later. EEOC v. Catastrophe Mgmt. Solutions, 2016 U.S. App. LEXIS 16918 at *41; Alex Janin, *What the Perception of 'Professional' Hair Means for Black Job Seekers*, Takepart.com, Apr. 13, 2016, http://www.takepart.com/article/2016/04/13/what-perception-professional-hair-means-black-job-seekers.

[xxxvi] Maryline Dossou, *Natural Hair vs. Corporate America: Why Are We Still Fighting This Battle?*, Ebony (Jul. 3, 2013), http://www.ebony.com/style/fighting-for-our-hair-in-corporate-america-032#axzz4Q5o3casI.

[xxxvii] Alex Janin, *What the Perception of 'Professional' Hair Means for Black Job Seekers*, Take part, (Apr. 13, 2016), http://www.takepart.com/article/2016/04/13/what-perception-professional-hair-means-black-job-seekers

[xxxviii] Barbara J. Flagg, *Fashioning a Title VII Remedy for Transparently White Subjective Decision-making.*, 104 Yale L.J. 2009, 2013 (1995).

[xxxix] Eatman v. UPS, 194 F. Supp. 2d 259, 259, 2002 (S.D.N.Y. 2002); Fagan v. National Cash Register Co., 481 F.2d 1115, 1115 (D.C. Cir. 1973).

[xl] Wigs: an artificial covering of hair for all or most of the head, of either synthetic or natural hair, worn to be stylish or more attractive. *Wig,* Dictionary.com, http://www.dictionary.com/browse/wig (last visited May 4, 2017).

[xli] Sabrina R. Perkins, *"Natural Hair In The Workplace: What Are Your Rights?" May Be A Viable Resource To Black Women*, Essence (Jul. 29, 2016), http://www.essence.com/2016/07/29/natural-hair-workplace-what-are-your-rights-may-be-viable-resource-black-women.

[xlii] Alex Janin, *What the Perception of 'Professional' Hair Means for Black Job Seekers*, Take part, (Apr. 13, 2016), http://www.takepart.com/article/2016/04/13/what-perception-professional-hair-means-black-job-seekers; According to the Bureau of Labor statistic report from September of 2016, "by race, Whites made up the majority of the labor force (79 percent)." United States Department of Labor, *Labor Force Characteristics by Race and Ethnicity, 2015*, Bureau of Labor Statistics (Sep. 2016), https://www.bls.gov/opub/reports/race-and-ethnicity/2015/home.htm.

[xliii] Maryline Dossou, *Natural Hair vs. Corporate America: Why Are We Still Fighting This Battle?*, Ebony (Jul. 3, 2013), http://www.ebony.com/style/fighting-for-our-hair-in-corporate-america-032#axzz4Q5o3casI.

[xliv] Cornrows: a type of braid, originating in Africa, in which a narrow strip of hair is plaited tightly against the scalp from front to back or from side to side." *Cornrow*, www.dictionary.com, http://www.dictionary.com/browse/cornrow (last visited Feb. 23, 2017); Dossou, *supra*, note 27.

[xlv] Maryline Dossou, *Natural Hair vs. Corporate America: Why Are We Still Fighting This Battle?*, Ebony (Jul. 3, 2013), http://www.ebony.com/style/fighting-for-our-hair-in-corporate-america-032#axzz4Q5o3casI.

[xlvi] Alex Janin, *What the Perception of 'Professional' Hair Means for Black Job Seekers*, Take part, (Apr. 13, 2016), http://www.takepart.com/article/2016/04/13/what-perception-professional-hair-means-black-job-seekers

[xlvii] Alex Janin, *What the Perception of 'Professional' Hair Means for Black Job Seekers*,

Take part, (Apr. 13, 2016), http://www.takepart.com/article/2016/04/13/what-perception-professional-hair-means-black-job-seekers

[xlviii] 42 U.S.C. §2000e-2; *See also* Imani Gandy, *Black Hair Discrimination Is Real—But Is It Against the Law?*, rewire news, (Apr 17, 2017, 4:58 PM), https://rewire.news/ablc/2017/04/17/black-hair-discrimination-real-but-is-it-against-law/ (showing that employers are more likely to favor hairstyles more comparable to White people and because the federal government is not required to follow the EEOC standards that prohibits discrimination based on hairstyles, therefore, employers are not in violation of any laws); *Mutable* characteristics are those characteristics that you are not born with, that can be changed or altered. EEOC v. Catastrophe Mgmt. Solutions, 852 F.3d 1018, 1030 (11th Cir. 2016).

[xlix] Alex Janin, *What the Perception of 'Professional' Hair Means for Black Job Seekers*, Take part, (Apr. 13, 2016), http://www.takepart.com/article/2016/04/13/what-perception-professional-hair-means-black-job-seekers

[l] Barbara J. Flagg, *Fashioning a Title VII Remedy for Transparently White Subjective Decision-making.*, 104 Yale L.J. 2009, 2013 (1995).

[li] Rumeana Jahangir, *How Does Black Hair Reflect Black History?*, BBC News (May 31, 2015), http://www.bbc.com/news/uk-england-merseyside-31438273; Since slavery, it has been thought that persons of a darker skin and with African features, including hair texture, only encompassed those of African descent. However, the term Black American has been commonly used to encompass both those who identify as Black and those of African descent. *Indivisible, African-Native American Lives in the Americas,* Smithsonian, *http://www.nmai.si.edu/exhibitions/indivisible/index.html (showing the coming together of African and Native Americans); Black Indians An American Story, Rich-Hemp Films, https://www.richheape.com/black-indians-american-story.htm (showing intermingling of African and Native Americans); see* Dania Santana, *What Is An Afro-Latina?#AmericanLatinos*, embracing diversity, http://embracingdiversity.us/what-is-an-afro-latina-black-latina/ (defining an Afro Latina as a person who has Black person who comes from Latin America or a person of African descent whose origin is from Latin America); *See* James Mooney, *Myths of the Cherokee, Nineteenth Annual Report, Bureau of American Ethnology, 1897-98* 233 (2015) (stating that as early as the late nineteenth century of the Nineteenth Annual Report of the Bureau of American Ethnology noted that a considerable proportion of the blood of the southern Negro [of the U.S.] is "unquestionably Indian"); *see* Muhammad, *supra* note 8.

[lii] Hot comb: a metal comb usually electrically heated for straightening or styling the hair. *Hot Comb*, merriam-webster.com, https://www.merriam-webster.com/dictionary/hot%20comb (last visited Feb. 23, 2017).

[liii] *Biography: Madam C.J. Walker*, biography, http://www.biography.com/people/madam-cj-walker-9522174; Henry Louis Gates, Jr., *Madam Walker, The First Black American Woman to Be a Self-Made Millionaire*, PBS, www.pbs.org, http://www.pbs.org/wnet/african-americans-many-rivers-to-cross/history/100-amazing-facts/madam-walker-the-first-black-american-woman-to-be-a-self-made-millionaire/.

[liv] Henry Louis Gates, Jr., *Madam Walker, The First Black American Woman to Be a Self-Made Millionaire*, PBS, www.pbs.org, http://www.pbs.org/wnet/african-americans-many-rivers-to-cross/history/100-amazing-facts/madam-walker-the-first-black-american-woman-to-be-a-self-made-millionaire; Antonia Opiah, *The Changing Business of Black Hair, a Potentially $500b Industry*, huffington post (Jan. 24, 2014, 10:53 AM), http://www.huffingtonpost.com/antonia-opiah/the-changing-business-of-_b_4650819.html.

[lv] Shelby Edwards, *Relaxer Hair Sales Continue Decline as Black Hair Industry Aimed to Be Worth Over $774 Million*, atlanta black star (July 29, 2015), http://atlantablackstar.com/2015/07/29/relaxer-hair-sales-continue-decline-as-black-hair-industry-aimed-to-be-worth-over-774-million/.

[lvi] Tamara E. Holmes, *The Industry That Black Women Built*, www.essence.com (Oct. 22, 2019), https://www.essence.com/news/money-career/business-black-beauty/ (last visited Aug. 23, 2020).

[lvii] Jenkins v. Blue Cross Mut. Hosp. Ins., Inc., 538 F.2d 164, 167-68, 169 (7th Cir. 1976); Chinwe, *The Natural Hair Movement in the '60s and '70s; How It Began and Why It Ended*, black girl long hair (Jan. 12, 2015), http://blackgirllonghair.com/2015/01/the-natural-hair-movement-in-the-60s-and-70s-how-it-began-and-why-it-ended/ (last visited July 25, 2020); To be discussed later, wearing hair in an Afro is protected under Title VII. *Jenkins, Inc.*, 538 F.2d at 167-68.

[lviii] Chinwe, *The Natural Hair Movement in the '60s and '70s; How It Began and Why It Ended*, black girl long hair (Jan. 12, 2015), http://blackgirllonghair.com/2015/01/the-natural-hair-movement-in-the-60s-and-70s-how-it-began-and-why-it-ended/ (last visited July 25, 2020).

[lix] *See* Chinwe, *The Natural Hair Movement in the '60s and '70s; How It Began and Why It Ended*, black girl long hair (Jan. 12, 2015), http://blackgirllonghair.com/2015/01/the-natural-hair-movement-in-the-60s-and-70s-how-it-began-and-why-it-ended/ (last visited July 25, 2020).

[lx] The Jheri Curl is often referred to as the curl kit is a "two-part application that consisted of a softener (often called a "rearranging cream") to loosen the hair and a solution to set the curls. The rearranging cream used pungent chemicals, causing the naturally tight curls to loosen and hang. The loose hair was then set on perm rods and a chemical solution was then added to the hair to permanently curl it." The curl, if not used with the activator solution, can cause hair to become dry and brittle. A touch up for the new growth roots of the hair is needed to maintain the style. *Black History Beauty Trend: The Jheri Curl*, fashion bomb daily (Feb. 2, 2010), http://fashionbombdaily.com/black-history-beauty-trend-the-jheri-curl/ (last visited July 25, 2020).

[lxi] Chinwe, *The Natural Hair Movement in the '60s and '70s; How It Began and Why It Ended*, black girl long hair (Jan. 12, 2015), http://blackgirllonghair.com/2015/01/the-natural-hair-movement-in-the-60s-and-70s-how-it-began-and-why-it-ended/ (last visited July 25, 2020).

[lxii] *See Discovering Our Roots: Do I Hate My Hair*, Thirsty Roots, http://thirstyroots.com/black-hair-history/discovering-our-roots-do-i-hate-my-hair (last visited Aug. 3, 2017); *see* Kristin Booker, *A History Of Black Hair In America*, Refinery29 (Feb. 21, 2014, 4:00 PM), http://www.refinery29.com/black-hair-history#slide-22; *see* Damon Young, *The Nappyheaded Black Male Revolution Is On*, TheRoot (Nov. 1, 2015, 3:00 AM), https://www.theroot.com/the-nappyheaded-black-male-revolution-is-on-1790861621 (last visited July 25, 2020).

[lxiii] 42 U.S.C. §2000e-2.

[lxiv] 42 U.S.C. §2000e-2.

[lxv] 42 U.S.C. §2000e-2; EEOC v. Catastrophe Mgmt. Solutions, 852 F.3d 1018, 1026 (11th Cir. 2016).

[lxvi] EEOC v. Catastrophe Mgmt. Solutions, 852 F.3d 1018, 1027 (11th Cir. 2016).

[lxvii] EEOC v. Catastrophe Mgmt. Solutions, 852 F.3d 1018, 1021 (11th Cir. 2016).

[lxviii] *About EEOC*, EEOC, https://www.eeoc.gov/eeoc/ (last visited Feb. 6, 2017).

[lxix] *U.S. Equal Employment Opportunity Commission, Prohibited Employment Policies/Practices: Dress Code*, EEOC, https://www.eeoc.gov/laws/practices/index.cfm (last visited Sept. 29, 2018).

[lxx] *U.S. Equal Employment Opportunity Commission, Prohibited Employment Policies/Practices: Dress Code*, EEOC, https://www.eeoc.gov/laws/practices/index.cfm (last visited Sept. 29, 2018).

[lxxi] *U.S. Equal Employment Opportunity Commission, Prohibited Employment Policies/Practices: Dress Code*, EEOC, https://www.eeoc.gov/laws/practices/index.cfm (last visited Sept. 29, 2018).

[lxxii] *U.S. Equal Employment Opportunity Commission, Prohibited Employment Policies/Practices: Dress Code*, EEOC, https://www.eeoc.gov/laws/practices/index.cfm (last visited Sept. 29, 2018).

[lxxiii] EEOC v. Catastrophe Mgmt. Solutions, 852 F.3d 1018, 1021 (11th Cir. 2016).

[lxxiv] *See generally* EEOC v. Catastrophe Mgmt. Solutions, 852 F.3d 1018, 1028 (11th Cir. 2016).

[lxxv] EEOC v. Catastrophe Mgmt. Solutions, 852 F.3d 1018, 1021 (11th Cir. 2016).

[lxxvi] EEOC v. Catastrophe Mgmt. Solutions, 852 F.3d 1018, 1031 (11th Cir. 2016).; Willingham v. Macon Telegraph Publ'g Co., 507 F.2d 1084 (5th Cir. 1975).

[lxxvii] Willingham v. Macon Telegraph Publ'g Co., 507 F.2d 1084 (5th Cir. 1975); *See generally Catastrophe Mgmt. Solutions*, 852 F.3d at 1028; The EEOC has updated their website to include their new stance on race discrimination to include hair texture. *Race/Color Discrimination*, U.S. Equal Employment Opportunity Commission, eeoc.gov, https://www.eeoc.gov/racecolor-discrimination (last visited Aug. 23, 2020).

[lxxviii] EEOC v. Catastrophe Mgmt. Solutions, 852 F.3d 1018, 1031 (11th Cir. 2016).

[lxxix] *See* Rogers v. Am. Airlines, Inc., 527 F. Supp. 231, 232 (S.D.N.Y. 1981); *see generally* EEOC v. Catastrophe Mgmt. Solutions, 852 F.3d 1018,1034 (11th Cir. 2016).

[lxxx] *Catastrop* EEOC v. Catastrophe Mgmt. Solutions, 852 F.3d 1018, 1034 (11th Cir. 2016).

[lxxxi] EEOC v. Catastrophe Mgmt. Solutions, 852 F.3d 1018, 1031 (11th Cir. 2016).

[lxxxii] Fagan v. National Cash Register Co., 481 F.2d 1115, 1115-16 (D.C. Cir. 1973).

[lxxxiii] Fagan v. National Cash Register Co., 481 F.2d 1115, 1119-21 (D.C. Cir. 1973).

[lxxxiv] Fagan v. National Cash Register Co., 481 F.2d 1115, 1119-21 (D.C. Cir. 1973).

[lxxxv] Fagan v. National Cash Register Co., 481 F.2d 1115, 1119-21 (D.C. Cir. 1973).

[lxxxvi] Fagan v. National Cash Register Co., 481 F.2d 1115, 1119-21 (D.C. Cir. 1973).

[lxxxvii] *Immutable* Characteristics: a characteristic determined solely by the accident of birth. It is a characteristic that you are born with. Board of Comm'rs v. Gustafson, 616 So. 2d 1165, 1167 (Fla. Dist. Ct. 1993) (quoting Frontiero v. Richardson, 411 U.S. 677, 686).

[lxxxviii] Fagan v. National Cash Register Co., 481 F.2d 1115, 1125 (D.C. Cir. 1973).

[lxxxix] Fagan v. National Cash Register Co., 481 F.2d 1115, 1126 (D.C. Cir. 1973).

[xc] Willingham v. Macon Telegraph Publ'g Co., 507 F.2d 1084, 1086 (5th Cir. 1975).

[xci] Willingham v. Macon Telegraph Publ'g Co., 507 F.2d 1084, 1087 (5th Cir. 1975).

[xcii] Willingham v. Macon Telegraph Publ'g Co., 507 F.2d 1084, 1086-87 (5th Cir. 1975).

[xciii] Willingham v. Macon Telegraph Publ'g Co., 507 F.2d 1084, 1091 (5th Cir. 1975).

[xciv] Willingham v. Macon Telegraph Publ'g Co., 507 F.2d 1084, 1088 (5th Cir. 1975).

[xcv] Willingham v. Macon Telegraph Publ'g Co., 507 F.2d 1084, 1091 (5th Cir. 1975).

[xcvi] Willingham v. Macon Telegraph Publ'g Co., 507 F.2d 1084, 1092 (5th Cir. 1975).

[xcvii] Rogers v. Am. Airlines, Inc., 527 F. Supp. 229, 231 (S.D.N.Y. 1981).

[xcviii] Rogers v. Am. Airlines, Inc., 527 F. Supp. 229, 233 (S.D.N.Y. 1981).

[xcix] The plaintiff asserted a Thirteenth Amendment claim but the court held that the claim failed because, "[t]hat provision prohibits practices that constitute a "badge of slavery" and unless a plaintiff alleges she does not have the option of leaving her job, does not support claims of racial discrimination in employment. The plaintiff argued that the style was, "historically, a fashion and style adopted by Black American women, reflective of cultural, historical essence of the Black women in American society." *Rog* Rogers v. Am. Airlines, Inc., 527 F. Supp. 229, 231 (S.D.N.Y. 1981) (quoting Davis v. Pepsi Cola Metropolitan Bottling Co., 18 F.E.P.

Cases 531, 533 (E.D.Pa.1978)).

[c] Rogers v. Am. Airlines, Inc., 527 F. Supp. 229, 231 (S.D.N.Y. 1981).

[ci] Rogers v. Am. Airlines, Inc., 527 F. Supp. 229, 232 (S.D.N.Y. 1981).

[cii] Rogers v. Am. Airlines, Inc., 527 F. Supp. 229, 232 (S.D.N.Y. 1981).

[ciii] Rogers v. Am. Airlines, Inc., 527 F. Supp. 229, 232 (S.D.N.Y. 1981).

[civ] Rogers v. Am. Airlines, Inc., 527 F. Supp. 229, 232 (S.D.N.Y. 1981); Garcia v. Gloor, 618 F.2d 264, 267-69 (5th Cir. 1980) (stating that "an evenhanded application of a reasonable grooming standard does not constitute racial discrimination" when an employee refuses to adhere to the policy).

[cv] Rogers v. Am. Airlines, Inc., 527 F. Supp. 229, 232 (S.D.N.Y. 1981); Garcia v. Gloor, 618 F.2d 264, 267-69 (5th Cir. 1980).

[cvi] Carswell v. Peachford Hosp., 1981 U.S. Dist. LEXIS 14562, *1 (N.D. Ga. 1981).

[cvii] Carswell v. Peachford Hosp., 1981 U.S. Dist. LEXIS 14562, *3 (N.D. Ga. 1981).

[cviii] Carswell v. Peachford Hosp., 1981 U.S. Dist. LEXIS 14562, *3 (N.D. Ga. 1981).

[cix] Carswell v. Peachford Hosp., 1981 U.S. Dist. LEXIS 14562, *3 (N.D. Ga. 1981).

[cx] Carswell v. Peachford Hosp., 1981 U.S. Dist. LEXIS 14562, *3 (N.D. Ga. 1981).

[cxi] Disparate Impact: claims filed by plaintiffs who have been discriminated against by policies in the workplace that are neutral on its face but tend to have a discriminatory impact on a constitutionally protected class. To be discussed further. 42 USCS § 2000e-2(k).

[cxii] Carswell v. Peachford Hosp., 1981 U.S. Dist. LEXIS 14562, *1 (N.D. Ga. 1981).

[cxiii] Carswell v. Peachford Hosp., 1981 U.S. Dist. LEXIS 14562, *5 (N.D. Ga. 1981); *Cf.* Garcia v. Gloor, 618 F.2d 264, 267-69 (5th Cir. 1980).

[cxiv] Carswell v. Peachford Hosp., 1981 U.S. Dist. LEXIS 14562, *6 (N.D. Ga. 1981).

[cxv] Carswell v. Peachford Hosp., 1981 U.S. Dist. LEXIS 14562, *8 (N.D. Ga. 1981).

[cxvi] McBride v. Lawstaf, Inc., No. CIV. A.1:96-CV-0196C, 1996 U.S. Dist. LEXIS 16190, at *3-4 (N.D. Ga. 1996).

[cxvii] McBride v. Lawstaf, Inc., No. CIV. A.1:96-CV-0196C, 1996 U.S. Dist. LEXIS 16190, at *3-4 (N.D. Ga. 1996).

[cxviii] McBride v. Lawstaf, Inc., No. CIV. A.1:96-CV-0196C, 1996 U.S. Dist. LEXIS 16190, at *3-4 (N.D. Ga. 1996).

[cxix] Hollins v. Atlantic Co., 188 F.3d 652, 656 (6th Cir. Ohio 1999).

[cxx] Hollins v. Atlantic Co., 188 F.3d 652, 655-56 (6th Cir. Ohio 1999).

[cxxi] Finger waves: "a method of setting hair by dampening with water or wave solution and forming waves or curls with the fingers and a comb." *Finger waves*, merrian-webster.com, https://www.merriam-webster.com/dictionary/finger%20wave (last visited May 4, 2017).

[cxxii] Hollins v. Atlantic Co., 188 F.3d 652, 655 (6th Cir. Ohio 1999).

[cxxiii] Hollins v. Atlantic Co., 188 F.3d 652, 656 (6th Cir. Ohio 1999).

[cxxiv] Hollins v. Atlantic Co., 188 F.3d 652, 660 (6th Cir. Ohio 1999).

[cxxv] Hollins v. Atlantic Co., 188 F.3d 652, 656-57 (6th Cir. Ohio 1999).

[cxxvi] Hollins v. Atlantic Co., 188 F.3d 652, 662-63 (6th Cir. Ohio 1999).

[cxxvii] Hollins v. Atlantic Co., 188 F.3d 652, 660 (6th Cir. Ohio 1999).

[cxxviii] Hollins v. Atlantic Co., 188 F.3d 652, 663 (6th Cir. Ohio 1999).

[cxxix] Lewis v. UPS, 2005 U.S. Dist. LEXIS 23488, *1-2 (N.D. Cal. 2005).

[cxxx] Lewis v. UPS, 2005 U.S. Dist. LEXIS 23488, *1-2 (N.D. Cal. 2005).

[cxxxi] Lewis v. UPS, 2005 U.S. Dist. LEXIS 23488, *10 (N.D. Cal. 2005).

[cxxxii] Lewis' claims were asserted for disability and religious discrimination not race discrimination. The court found that if the employer knew that the dreadlocks were being worn for religious reasons and the employee suffered harassment because of his religious beliefs the employee could have asserted a claim religious discrimination claim. The court also determined that there was no genuine issue of material fact on his disability claim. Lewis v. UPS, 2005 U.S. Dist. LEXIS 23488, *10-12, *13-14 (N.D. Cal. 2005).

[cxxxiii] Lewis v. UPS, 2005 U.S. Dist. LEXIS 23488, *10 (N.D. Cal. 2005).

[cxxxiv] Lewis v. UPS, 2005 U.S. Dist. LEXIS 23488, *11 (N.D. Cal. 2005).

[cxxxv] Lewis v. UPS, 2005 U.S. Dist. LEXIS 23488, *11 (N.D. Cal. 2005).

[cxxxvi] *Pitts v. Wild Adventures*, Inc., 2008 U.S. Dist. LEXIS 34119, *3 (M.D. Ga. 2008).

[cxxxvii] *Pitts v. Wild Adventures*, Inc., 2008 U.S. Dist. LEXIS 34119, *3 (M.D. Ga. 2008).

[cxxxviii] *Pitts v. Wild Adventures*, Inc., 2008 U.S. Dist. LEXIS 34119, *4-5 (M.D. Ga. 2008).

[cxxxix] *Pitts v. Wild Adventures*, Inc., 2008 U.S. Dist. LEXIS 34119, *4-5 (M.D. Ga. 2008).

[cxl] *Pitts v. Wild Adventures*, Inc., 2008 U.S. Dist. LEXIS 34119, *4-5 (M.D. Ga. 2008).

[cxli] *Pitts v. Wild Adventures*, Inc., 2008 U.S. Dist. LEXIS 34119, *10 (M.D. Ga. 2008).

[cxlii] *Pitts v. Wild Adventures*, Inc., 2008 U.S. Dist. LEXIS 34119, *15 (M.D. Ga. 2008).

[cxliii] *Pitts v. Wild Adventures*, Inc., 2008 U.S. Dist. LEXIS 34119, *18 (M.D. Ga. 2008).

[cxliv] *See Pitts v. Wild Adventures*, Inc., 2008 U.S. Dist. LEXIS 34119, *19 (M.D. Ga. 2008); Willingham v. Macon Telegraph Publishing Co., 507 F.2d 1084, 1092 (5th Cir. 1975).

[cxlv] *Pitts v. Wild Adventures*, Inc., 2008 U.S. Dist. LEXIS 34119, *19 (M.D. Ga. 2008).

[cxlvi] Eatman v. UPS, 194 F. Supp. 2d 259 (S.D.N.Y. 2002).

[cxlvii]Beanie: a skullcap, often brightly colored, worn especially by children and by college freshmen, especially in the 1940s. *Beanie*, Dictionary.com, https://www.dictionary.com/browse/beanie?s=ts (last visited Sep. 20, 2018). Skully- a type of hat often referred to as a beanie. Skullyhat.com, http://skullyhat.com (last visited May 4, 2017).

[cxlviii] Eatman v. UPS, 194 F. Supp. 2d 259-60 (S.D.N.Y. 2002).

[cxlix] Eatman v. UPS, 194 F. Supp. 2d 259-60 (S.D.N.Y. 2002).

[cl] Eatman v. UPS, 194 F. Supp. 2d 259 (S.D.N.Y. 2002).

[cli] Disparate Impact: claims filed by plaintiffs who have been discriminated against by policies in the workplace that are neutral on its face but tend to have a discriminatory impact on a protected class. To be discussed further. *See infra* at note 154. 42 USCS § 2000e-2(k) (setting forth burden of proof for disparate impact cases).

[clii] Eatman v. UPS, 194 F. Supp. 2d 259 (S.D.N.Y. 2002).

[cliii] EEOC v. Catastrophe Mgmt. Solutions, 852 F.3d 1018 (11th Cir. 2016).

[cliv] EEOC v. Catastrophe Mgmt. Solutions, 852 F.3d 1018, 1021 (11th Cir. 2016).

[clv] EEOC v. Catastrophe Mgmt. Solutions, 852 F.3d 1018, 1022 (11th Cir. 2016).

[clvi] EEOC v. Catastrophe Mgmt. Solutions, 852 F.3d 1018, 1023 (11th Cir. 2016).

[clvii] EEOC v. Catastrophe Mgmt. Solutions, 852 F.3d 1018, 1023 (11th Cir. 2016).

[clviii] "Under a disparate treatment theory, (1) [plaintiff] must establish a prima facie case; (2) [employer] would then be required to offer a legitimate, nondiscriminatory reason for the policy; and (3) [employee] would then have the opportunity to establish that the proffered reason was pretextual. Proof of discriminatory intent is an essential element of [plaintiffs'] prima facie case under a disparate treatment theory, although intent can in some situations be inferred from the mere fact of differences in treatment." Giles v. Ireland, 742 F.2d 1366, 1374 (11th Cir. Ala. 1984).

[clix] EEOC v. Catastrophe Mgmt. Solutions, 852 F.3d 1018, 1025 (11th Cir. 2016). The EEOC cited *Young v. UPS*, a case where the court used a burden shifting framework that puts the burden on the employer to show that there is a legitimate nondiscriminatory reason for policy practices, which does not attach intentional harms to members of a protected class shown in a disparate impact case. EEOC v. Catastrophe Mgmt. Solutions, 852 F.3d 1018, 1024 (11th Cir. 2016).

[clx] EEOC v. Catastrophe Mgmt. Solutions, 852 F.3d 1018, 1025 (11th Cir. 2016). (citing *Young*, 135 S. Ct. 1338, 1350 (U.S. 2015)).

[clxi] EEOC v. Catastrophe Mgmt. Solutions, 852 F.3d 1018, 1025-26 (11th Cir. 2016).. Typically, disparate impact claims are filed by plaintiffs who have been discriminated against by policies in the workplace that are neutral on its face but tend to have a discriminatory impact on a constitutionally protected class. The complaining party must show that the responding party, usually the employer, refused to adopt an alternative employment practice that would not have the effect of discriminating or that such practice was a business necessity. EEOC v. Joe's Stone Crab, Inc., 220 F.3d 1263, 1268 (11th Cir. Fla. 2000).

[clxii] EEOC v. Catastrophe Mgmt. Solutions, 852 F.3d 1018, 1025 (11th Cir. 2016).

[clxiii] EEOC v. Catastrophe Mgmt. Solutions, 852 F.3d 1018, 1022 (11th Cir. 2016).

[clxiv] *See* EEOC v. Catastrophe Mgmt. Solutions, 852 F.3d 1018, 1022 (11th Cir. 2016).

[clxv] *See* EEOC v. Catastrophe Mgmt. Solutions, 852 F.3d 1018, 1034 (11th Cir. 2016).

[clxvi] *See* EEOC v. Catastrophe Mgmt. Solutions, 852 F.3d 1018, 1034 (11th Cir. 2016).

[clxvii] *See* EEOC v. Catastrophe Mgmt. Solutions, 852 F.3d 1018, 1034 (11th Cir. 2016).

[clxviii] *Catastrophe Mgmt. Solutions*, 852 F.3d at 1033.

[clxix] *Id.*

[clxx] Wendy Greene, Title VII: What's Hair (and Other Race-Based Characteristics) Got to Do With It, 79 U. Colo. L. Rev. 1355, 1364-65 (2008).

[clxxi] EEOC v Catastrophe Mgmt. Solutions, 876 F.3d 1274, 1273 (11th Cir. 2017).

[clxxii] *See* EEOC v Catastrophe Mgmt. Solutions, 876 F.3d 1274, 1274 (11th Cir. 2017).

[clxxiii] EEOC v Catastrophe Mgmt. Solutions, 876 F.3d 1274, 1275 (11th Cir. 2017).

[clxxiv] EEOC v Catastrophe Mgmt. Solutions, 876 F.3d 1274, 1277 (11th Cir. 2017).

[clxxv] Price Waterhouse v Hopkins, 490 U.S. 228, 235 (1989).

[clxxvi] Price Waterhouse v Hopkins, 490 U.S. 228, 235 (1989).

[clxxvii] EEOC v Catastrophe Mgmt. Solutions, 876 F.3d 1274, 1275 (11th Cir. 2017).

[clxxviii] EEOC v Catastrophe Mgmt. Solutions, 876 F.3d 1274, 1275 (11th Cir. 2017).

[clxxix] EEOC v Catastrophe Mgmt. Solutions, 876 F.3d 1274, 1284 (11th Cir. 2017).

[clxxx] EEOC v Catastrophe Mgmt. Solutions, 876 F.3d 1274, 1285 (11th Cir. 2017).

[clxxxi] EEOC v Catastrophe Mgmt. Solutions, 876 F.3d 1274, 1285 (11th Cir. 2017).

[clxxxii] EEOC v Catastrophe Mgmt. Solutions, 876 F.3d 1274, 1286 (11th Cir. 2017).

[clxxxiii] EEOC v Catastrophe Mgmt. Solutions, 876 F.3d 1274, 1287 (11th Cir. 2017).

[clxxxiv] EEOC v Catastrophe Mgmt. Solutions, 876 F.3d 1274, 1288 (11th Cir. 2017).

[clxxxv] EEOC v Catastrophe Mgmt. Solutions, 876 F.3d 1274, 1276 (11th Cir. 2017).

[clxxxvi] EEOC v Catastrophe Mgmt. Solutions, 876 F.3d 1274, 1289 (11th Cir. 2017). Pseudoscience- a system of theories, assumptions, and methods erroneously regarded as scientific. Pseudoscience, merriam-webster.com, https://www.merriam-webster.com/dictionary/pseudoscience (last visited June 27, 2020).

[clxxxvii] EEOC v Catastrophe Mgmt. Solutions, 138 S. Ct. (2018).

[clxxxviii] Ironically, one has to comb their hair to achieve the afro look.

[clxxxix] Jenkins v. Blue Cross Mut. Hosp. Ins., Inc., 538 F.2d 164, 167-68 (7th Cir. 1976).

[cxc] Jenkins v. Blue Cross Mut. Hosp. Ins., Inc., 538 F.2d 164, 168 (7th Cir. 1976).

[cxci] Hollins v. Atlantic Co., 188 F.3d 652, 660 (6th Cir. Ohio 1999).

[cxcii] *See* O'Loughlin v. Pinchback, 579 So. 2d 788, 791 (Fla. Dist. Ct. App. 1991).

[cxciii] Transatlantic Slave Trade: "the biggest deportation in history and a determining factor in the world economy of the 18th century. Millions of Africans were torn from their homes, deported to the American continent and sold as slaves." *Transatlantic Slave Trade*, UNESCO, http://www.unesco.org/new/en/social-and-human-sciences/themes/slave-route/transatlantic-slave-trade/ (last visited February 14, 2017).

[cxciv] Rumeana Jahangir, *How Does Black Hair Reflect Black History?*, BBC News (May 31, 2015), http://www.bbc.com/news/uk-england-merseyside-31438273.

[cxcv] EEOC v. Catastrophe Mgmt. Solutions, 852 F.3d 1018, 1022 (11th Cir. 2016).

[cxcvi] EEOC v. Catastrophe Mgmt. Solutions, 852 F.3d 1018, 1022 (11th Cir. 2016).

[cxcvii] Rumeana Jahangir, *How Does Black Hair Reflect Black History?*, BBC News (May 31, 2015), http://www.bbc.com/news/uk-england-merseyside-31438273.

[cxcviii] Ayana D. Byrd & Lori L. Tharps, Hair Story: Untangling the Roots of Black Hair in America 13 (2001).

[cxcix] Ayana D. Byrd & Lori L. Tharps, Hair Story: Untangling the Roots of Black Hair in America 13 (2001).

[cc] *See* Rumeana Jahangir, *How Does Black Hair Reflect Black History?*, BBC News (May 31, 2015), http://www.bbc.com/news/uk-england-merseyside-31438273.

[cci] *See* Rumeana Jahangir, *How Does Black Hair Reflect Black History?*, BBC News (May 31, 2015), http://www.bbc.com/news/uk-england-merseyside-31438273.

[ccii] Ian F. Haney Lopez, *The Social Construction of Race: Some Observations on Illusion, Fabrication, and Choice*, 29 Harv. C.R.-C.L. L. Rev. 1, 7 (1994).

[cciii] According to Fletcher, the genotypical characteristics of each race are passed on through genetic codes from parents to children which is then observable through phenotypical expressions which are visually seen in a person's appearance such as skin tone, eye color, skull density, and texture of one's hair. This idea is also evidenced in an online article published by Brown defining, "phenotype is the constellation of observable traits; genotype is

the genetic endowment of the individual." Interview with Andre L. Fletcher, Former Biology Laboratory Researcher, Texas Southern University Biology B.S., (Apr. 8, 2017); Phenotype and Genotype, biomed.brown.edu, https://biomed.brown.edu/Courses/BIO48/5.Geno.Pheno.HTML (last visited Apr. 8, 2017).

[cciv] *Other Traits*, The Tech. Museum of Innovation (April 25, 2005), http://genetics.thetech.org/ask/ask107;
What Is Natural Hair?, Blackhair.about.com, http://blackhair.about.com/od/glossary/g/natural.htm (Last Updated May 06, 2016).

[ccv] *Other Traits*, The Tech. Museum of Innovation (April 25, 2005), http://genetics.thetech.org/ask/ask107

[ccvi] *Other Traits*, The Tech. Museum of Innovation (April 25, 2005), http://genetics.thetech.org/ask/ask107

[ccvii] The hair texture difference is due to, "cross section [being] elliptical or almost flat and ribbon-like in some cases. This means that there is more strength and rigidity to the fiber across the area of greatest cross section but the hair is much more pliable across the narrow section. This results in the curls of hair all naturally flexing and coiling along the ribbon while there is little or no coiling from side to side," as opposed to say Caucasian hair where the, "fiber[s] can be circular or oval in cross section," and more dense than African American hair. *Ethnic Differences in Hair Fiber and Hair Follicles*, keratin.com, http://www.keratin.com/aa/aa002.shtml (last visited July 25, 2020).

[ccviii] *Ethnic Differences in Hair Fiber and Hair Follicles*, keratin.com, http://www.keratin.com/aa/aa002.shtml (last visited July 25, 2020).

[ccix] EEOC v. Catastrophe Mgmt. Solutions, 852 F.3d 1018, 1027 (11th Cir. 2016); The idea of using biological differences is in direct opposition of the view of courts and legislatures when defining race for the enactment and enforcement of laws such as Title VII. *Contra*, Rhonda V. Magee Andrews, *The Third Reconstruction: An Alternative to Race Consciousness and Colorblindness in Post-Slavery America*, 54 Ala. L. Rev. 515, 515 (2003) (citing the opinion in the *Catastrophe Mgmt. Solutions* case, identifying race as not being biological but as "an emerging contemporary understanding of the meaning of race.")

[ccx] *What Relaxers Really Do To Your Hair*, BlackDoctor.org, http://blackdoctor.org/216545/what-relaxers-really-do-to-your-hair__trashed/2/.

[ccxi] *Hair Straightening: The Hidden Dangers*, feel good style, http://feelgoodstyle.com/2011/03/17/hair-straightening/ (last visited May 4, 2017); Chime Edwards, *Real Talk About Heat Damage*, essence (Sep. 29, 2015), http://www.essence.com/2015/09/29/real-talk-about-heat-damage (last visited July 26, 2020).

[ccxii] *Weaves vs Extensions*, Black Hair Media, http://blackhairmedia.com/weave-and-extension/weaves-vs-extensions-2/.

[ccxiii] Traction Alopecia: "hair loss and balding from the pulling and excess weight." Orly Avitzur, M.D., *The Dangers of Hair Extensions: The Beauty Trend Can Cause Headaches, Baldness, and Allergic Reactions*, consumer reports (Feb. 2013), http://www.consumerreports.org/cro/2013/02/the-dangers-of-hair-extensions/index.htm ast visited July 26, 2020).

[ccxiv] Orly Avitzur, M.D., *The Dangers of Hair Extensions: The Beauty Trend Can Cause Headaches, Baldness, and Allergic Reactions*, consumer reports (Feb. 2013), http://www.consumerreports.org/cro/2013/02/the-dangers-of-hair-extensions/index.htm ast visited July 26, 2020).

[ccxv] Synthetic hair: "extensions [that] are the first choice for many women, as they are affordable, long-lasting and low maintenance. Created from plastic fibers, these extensions are created in straight or curly styles and require little upkeep to maintain the look, which will not be affected by humidity or rain." Pamela Vanderwerf, *Synthetic Vs. Human Hair Extensions*, livestrong (Jul. 18, 2017), http://www.livestrong.com/article/66031-synthetic-vs.-human-hair-extensions/.

[ccxvi] Human Hair: "Human hair destined for hair extensions is obtained from many different countries, including Russia, China, Brazil, Peru and Malaysia. Human hair is classified as Remy for its uniform quality, with strands all facing the same directions, and it is defined as virgin if the strands have not been colored or permed." *Id.*

[ccxvii] Janice Jackson, *Understand the Dangers of Using Synthetic Hair Before You Buy It* (June 25, 2012), http://worldhairextensions.com/blog/general/understand-the-dangers-of-using-synthetic-hair-before-you-buy-it (last visited July 26, 2020).

[ccxviii] *What Relaxers Really Do To Your Hair*, BlackDoctor.org, http://blackdoctor.org/216545/what-relaxers-really-do-to-your-hair__trashed/2/.

[ccxix] Scarring Alopecia: permanent hair loss, that is impossible to correct. *What Relaxers Really Do To Your Hair*, BlackDoctor.org, http://blackdoctor.org/216545/what-relaxers-really-do-to-your-hair__trashed/2/.

[ccxx] "The main ingredient of lye relaxers, sodium hydroxide; no-lye relaxers which contain calcium hydroxide and guanidine carbonate; and thio relaxers which contain thioglycolic acid salts." Lauren A. Wise, Julie R. Palmer, David Reich, Yvette C. Cozier & Lynn Rosenberg, *Hair Relaxer Use and Risk of Uterine Leiomyomata in African-American Women*, 175.5 Am. J. of Epidemiology 432–440 (2012).

[ccxxi] Uterine leiomyomata or Uterine Fibriods: "are tumors of the myometrium that are responsive to estrogens and progesterone. Although benign, uterine leiomyomata are associated with significant gynecologic morbidity and are the leading indication for hysterectomy in the United States." Studies are continuing on the relation of relaxers and uterine fibroids in African American women. Lauren A. Wise, Julie R. Palmer, David Reich, Yvette C. Cozier & Lynn Rosenberg, *Hair Relaxer Use and Risk of Uterine Leiomyomata in African-American Women*, 175.5 Am. J. of Epidemiology 432–440 (2012).

[ccxxii] Lauren A. Wise, Julie R. Palmer, David Reich, Yvette C. Cozier & Lynn Rosenberg, *Hair Relaxer Use and Risk of Uterine Leiomyomata in African-American Women*, 175.5 Am. J. of Epidemiology 432–440 (2012).

[ccxxiii] "[Hair] [e]xtensions can cost as low as $300 (depending on your geographical area) and go up to $10,000. H. Fields Grenee, *What Spending A Half A Trillion Dollars on Hair Care and Weaves Says About Us*, madamenoire (May 11, 2011), http://madamenoire.com/57134/what-spending-a-half-a-trillion-dollars-on-hair-care-and-weaves-says-about-us/ (last visited July 26, 2020).

[ccxxiv] *Black Women Avoiding Exercise To Maintain Hairstyles: Study*, huffington post (Feb. 17, 2013), http://www.huffingtonpost.com/2012/12/18/black-women-hair-avoid-exercise_n_2321539.html (last visited July 26, 2020).

[ccxxv] Keys v. Continental Illinois Nat'l Bank & Trust Co., 357 F. Supp. 376, 377 (N.D. Ill. 1973).

[ccxxvi] Pseudofolliculitis Barbae is the formation of small or large bumps on the cheeks, chin, jawline, neck, under the chin and areas and the scalp that occurs commonly with tightly curled hair. "The cause of pseudofolliculitis barbae is the hair emerging from the curved follicle, which grows almost parallel to the skin surface (instead of away from the skin), and then curves inward again. The inward-curving hair punctures the skin, causing an inflammatory reaction, irritation, pain and unsightly bumps." Dr. Susan Taylor, *Skin Care Tips for Men With Brown Skin*, Brownskin.net (2008), http://www.brownskin.net/men.html (last visited July 26, 2020).

[ccxxvii] ." Dr. Susan Taylor, *Skin Care Tips for Men With Brown Skin*, Brownskin.net (2008), http://www.brownskin.net/men.html (last visited July 26, 2020).

[ccxxviii] ." Dr. Susan Taylor, *Skin Care Tips for Men With Brown Skin*, Brownskin.net (2008), http://www.brownskin.net/men.html (last visited July 26, 2020).

[ccxxix] ." Dr. Susan Taylor, *Skin Care Tips for Men With Brown Skin*, Brownskin.net (2008), http://www.brownskin.net/men.html (last visited July 26, 2020).

[ccxxx] Bradley v. Pizzaco of Nebraska, Inc., 7 F.3d 795, 796 (8th Cir. Neb. 1993).

[ccxxxi] Bradley v. Pizzaco of Nebraska, Inc., 7 F.3d 795, 796 (8th Cir. Neb. 1993).

[ccxxxii] Bradley v. Pizzaco of Nebraska, Inc., 7 F.3d 795, 798-99 (8th Cir. Neb. 1993).

[ccxxxiii] Bradley v. Pizzaco of Nebraska, Inc., 7 F.3d 795, 798-99 (8th Cir. Neb. 1993).; *Cf.* Keys v. Continental Illinois Nat'l Bank & Trust Co., 357 F. Supp. 376, 377 (N.D. Ill. 1973). Courts have neglected to find constitutional violations of where plaintiffs sought constitutional protections when wearing facial hair as symbolism of black pride and beauty.

[ccxxxiv] Bradley v. Pizzaco of Nebraska, Inc., 7 F.3d 795, 798-99 (8th Cir. Neb. 1993).

[ccxxxv] EEOC v. Trailways, Inc., 530 F. Supp. 54, 59 (D. Colo. 1981).

[ccxxxvi] EEOC v. Trailways, Inc., 530 F. Supp. 54, 59 (D. Colo. 1981).

[ccxxxvii] Dr. Susan Taylor, *Skin Care Tips for Men With Brown Skin*, Brownskin.net (2008), http://www.brownskin.net/men.html (last visited July 26, 2020).

[ccxxxviii] D.C. Code § 2-1401.01.

[ccxxxix] Estenos v. PAHO/WHO-FCU, 952 A.2d 878, 887 (D.C. 2008) (quoting § 2-1401.01).

[ccxl] Estenos v. PAHO/WHO-FCU, 952 A.2d 878, 887 (D.C. 2008) (quoting § 2-1401.01).

[ccxli] D.C. CODE §2-1401.02 (22).

[ccxlii] Fox v. Giaccia, 424 F. Supp. 2d 1, 7 (D.D.C. 2006).

[ccxliii] Fox v. Giaccia, 424 F. Supp. 2d 1, 7 (D.D.C. 2006).

[ccxliv] Fox v. Giaccia, 424 F. Supp. 2d 1, 7 (D.D.C. 2006).

[ccxlv] *DC City Profile – Population*, neighborhood info dc, http://www.neighborhoodinfodc.org/city/Nbr_prof_city.html (last visited Jan. 31, 2017).

[ccxlvi] *DC City Profile – Population, supra*, note 221.

[ccxlvii] *See* Alison Dundes Renteln, The Cultural Defense, 140-142 (2005) (book cites to *Pamela L. Mitchell v. J.W. Marriott Hotel, Inc, and Marriott Corporation* (1988), case settled).

[ccxlviii] *See* Alison Dundes Renteln, The Cultural Defense, 141 (2005) (book cites to *Pamela L. Mitchell v. J.W. Marriott Hotel, Inc, and Marriott Corporation* (1988), case settled).

[ccxlix] Alison Dundes Renteln, The Cultural Defense, 140-142 (2005) (book cites to *Pamela L. Mitchell v. J.W. Marriott Hotel, Inc, and Marriott Corporation* (1988), case settled).

[ccl] *See* Alison Dundes Renteln, The Cultural Defense, 140-142 (2005) (book cites to *Pamela L. Mitchell v. J.W. Marriott Hotel, Inc, and Marriott Corporation* (1988), case settled).

[ccli] *See* Alison Dundes Renteln, The Cultural Defense, 140-142 (2005) (book cites to *Pamela L. Mitchell v. J.W. Marriott Hotel, Inc, and Marriott Corporation* (1988), case settled).

[cclii] *See* Alison Dundes Renteln, supra note 223 at 141-42. (citing *Tatum & Parahoo v. Hyatt* (1988)).

[ccliii] *See* Alison Dundes Renteln, supra note 223 at 141-42. (citing *Tatum & Parahoo v. Hyatt* (1988)).

[ccliv] *See* Alison Dundes Renteln, supra note 223 at 141-42. (citing *Tatum & Parahoo v. Hyatt* (1988)).

[cclv] *See* Alison Dundes Renteln, supra note 223 at 142. (citing *Tatum & Parahoo v. Hyatt* (1988)).

[cclvi] *See* Alison Dundes Renteln, supra note 223 at 141-42. (citing *Tatum & Parahoo v. Hyatt*

(1988)).

[cclvii] Florida Lime & Avocado Growers, Inc. v. Paul, 373 U.S. 141, 141 (U.S. 1963).

[cclviii] XpertHR Employment Law Manual 2356 (2017).

[cclix] XpertHR Employment Law Manual 2356 (2017).

[cclx] XpertHR Employment Law Manual 2356 (2017).

[cclxi] XpertHR Employment Law Manual 2356 (2017).

[cclxii] XpertHR Employment Law Manual 2356 (2017).

[cclxiii] XpertHR Employment Law Manual 2356 (2017).

[cclxiv] Rogers v. Am. Airlines, Inc., 527 F. Supp. 229, 233 (S.D.N.Y. 1981); *See* Albertson's, Inc. v. Wash. State Human Rights Com., 14 Wn. App. 697, 702 (Wash. Ct. App. 1976); *See* XpertHR Employment Law Manual 2356 (2017).

[cclxv] Phil Willon, Alexa Diaz, *California becomes first state to ban discrimination based on one's natural hair*, latimes.com, (July 3, 2019), https://www.latimes.com/local/lanow/la-pol-ca-natural-hair-discrimination-bill-20190703-story.html (last visited July 26, 2020).

[cclxvi] Dove is a personal care product line. Dove, dove.com, https://www.dove.com/us/en/home.html (last visited March 28, 2020).

[cclxvii] The National Urban League works to provide economic empowerment, educational opportunities and the guarantee of civil rights for the underserved in America. *What we do*, The National Urban League, https://nul.org (last visited May 28, 2020).

[cclxviii] Color of Change is an organize dedicated to responding to injustices around the world. About, colorofchange.org, https://colorofchange.org/about/ (last visited July 26, 2020).

[cclxix] Western Center of Law & Poverty is dedicated to serving the interest of people experiencing poverty. About Western Center, Western Center of Law & Poverty, wclp.org, https://wclp.org/about-wclp/ (last visited July 26, 2020).

[cclxx] Dove: The Crown Research Study, static1.squarespace.com https://static1.squarespace.com/static/5edc69fd622c36173f56651f/t/5edeaa2fe5ddef345e087361/1591650865168/Dove_research_brochure2020_FINAL3.pdf (last visited July 26, 2020).

[cclxxi] Dove: The Crown Research Study, static1.squarespace.com https://static1.squarespace.com/static/5edc69fd622c36173f56651f/t/5edeaa2fe5ddef345e087361/1591650865168/Dove_research_brochure2020_FINAL3.pdf (last visited July 26, 2020).

[cclxxii] *About*, The Crown Act, thecrownact.com, https://www.thecrownact.com/about (last visited July 26, 2020);.

[cclxxiii] Danielle Meadows, Gov. Ricketts vetoes hair discrimination bill, 3newsnow.com, https://www.3newsnow.com/news/local-news/gov-ricketts-vetoes-hair-discrimination-bill (Posted at 5:44 PM, Aug 15, 2020 and last updated 6:27 PM, Aug 15, 2020).

[cclxxiv] Danielle Meadows, Gov. Ricketts vetoes hair discrimination bill, 3newsnow.com, https://www.3newsnow.com/news/local-news/gov-ricketts-vetoes-hair-discrimination-bill (Posted at 5:44 PM, Aug 15, 2020 and last updated 6:27 PM, Aug 15, 2020).

[cclxxv] "Make America Great" idea taken from the (then) 2016 Republican Candidate, President Donald J. Trump's Campaign Slogan.

Bibliography: My Hair is Professional TOO!

Cases

1. EEOC v. Catastrophe Mgmt. Solutions, 138 S. Ct. (2018).
2. EEOC v. Catastrophe Mgmt. Solutions, 876 F.3d 1274, 1273 (11th Cir. 2017).
3. EEOC v. Catastrophe Mgmt. Solutions, 2016 U.S. App. LEXIS 16918, *22 (11th Cir. Ala. 2016).
4. Estenos v. PAHO/WHO-FCU, 952 A.2d 887, 887 (D.C. 2008).
5. Pitts v. Wild Adventures, Inc., 2008 U.S. Dist. LEXIS 34119, *3 (M.D. Ga. 2008).
6. Willingham v. Macon Tel. Pub. Co., 507 F.2d at 1084, citing Thomas v. Chertoff, 2008 EEOPUB LEXIS 3977, *1-2, (E.E.O.C. 2008).
7. Fox v. Giaccia, 424 F. Supp. 2d 1, 7, 2006 U.S. Dist. LEXIS 17051, *7 (D.D.C. 2006).
8. Eatman v. UPS, 194 F. Supp. 2d 259, 259, 2002 (S.D.N.Y. 2002).
9. EEOC v. Joe's Stone Crab, Inc., 220 F.3d 1263, 1268 (11th Cir. Fla. 2000).
10. Hollins v. Atlantic Co., 188 F.3d 652, 656 (6th Cir. Ohio 1999).
11. Harper v. Blockbuster Entm't Corp., 139 F.3d 1385, 1389 (11th Cir. Fla. 1998) certiorari denied, 119 S. Ct. 509, 525 (U.S. 1998).
12. McBride v. Lawstaf, Inc., No. CIV. A.1:96-CV-0196C, 1996 U.S. Dist. LEXIS 16190, at *3-4 (N.D. Ga. 1996).
13. Kelly v. K.D. Constr., 866 F. Supp. 1406, 1410 (S.D. Fla. 1994).
14. Board of Comm'rs v. Gustafson, 616 So. 2d 1165, 1167 (Fla. Dist. Ct. 1993).
15. Bradley v. Pizzaco of Nebraska, Inc., 7 F.3d 795, 796 (8th Cir. Neb. 1993).
16. Price Waterhouse v. Hopkins, 490 U.S. 228, 235 (1989).

17. Giles v. Ireland, 742 F.2d 1366, 1374 (11th Cir. Ala. 1984).
18. Rogers v. Am. Airlines, Inc., 527 F. Supp. 231, 232 (S.D.N.Y. 1981).
19. Carswell v. Peachford Hospital, 1981 U.S. Dist. LEXIS 14562, *1 (N.D. Ga. 1981).
20. EEOC v. Trailways, Inc., 530 F. Supp. 54, 59 (D. Colo. 1981).
21. Garcia v. Gloor, 618 F.2d 264 (5th Cir. 1980).
22. Jenkins v. Blue Cross Mut. Hosp. Ins., Inc., 538 F.2d 167-68, 169 (7th Cir. 1976).
23. Wash. v. Davis, 426 U.S. 229, 270 (U.S. 1976).
24. Fagan v. National Cash Register Co., 481 F.2d 1125, 1126 (D.D.C. 1973).
25. Florida Lime & Avocado Growers, Inc. v. Paul, 373 U.S. 141, 178 (U.S. 1963).
26. Keys v. Continental Illinois Nat'l Bank & Trust Co., 357 F. Supp. 376, 377 (N.D. Ill. 1973).

Statutes

1. U.S.C. §2000e-2.
2. Fla. Stat. § 760.10;
3. S.B. 1368 1992 Sess. (Fl. 1992).
4. D.C. Code § 2-1401.01
5. D.C. Code § 2-1401.02
6. D.C. Code § 2-1401.11.
7. 42 USCS § 2000e-2(k).
8. D.C. Code § 2-1401.01
9. 42 U.S.C. §2000e-2.

Treatises

1. Discrimination: Race, National Origin, Gender, Religion and Age, §2.21 (EMPL. L. 19944).
2. XpertHR Employment Law Manual 2356 (2017).

Scholarly Articles

1. Barbara J. Flagg, ARTICLE: Fashioning a Title VII Remedy for Transparently White Subjective Decisionmaking., 104 YALE L.J. (2009).
2. Wendy Greene, Article: Title VII: What's Hair (and Other Race-Based Characteristics) Got to Do With It, 79 U. Colo. L. Rev. 1355, 1364-65 (2008).
3. Ian F. Haney Lopez, Article: The Social Construction of Race: Some Observations on Illusion, Fabrication, and Choice, 29 Harv. C.R.-C.L. L. Rev. 1, 7 (1994).
4. Rhonda V. Magee Andrews, The Third Reconstruction: An Alternative to Race Consciousness and Colorblindness in Post-Slavery America, 54 Ala. L. Rev. 515, 515 (2003).

Books

1. Ayana D. Byrd & Lori L. Tharps, Hair Story: Untangling the Roots of Black Hair in America, 13, (2001).
2. Alison Dundes Renteln, The Cultural Defense, 140-142 (2005).

Online Resources

1. Phil Willon, Alexa Diaz, California becomes first state to ban discrimination based on one's natural hair, LATIMES.COM, (July 3, 2019), https://www.latimes.com/local/lanow/la-pol-ca-natural-hair-discrimination-bill-20190703-story.html (last visited July 26, 2020).
2. Dove, DOVE.COM, https://www.dove.com/us/en/home.html (last visited March 28, 2020).
3. About, COLOROFCHANGE.ORG, https://colorofchange.org/about/ (last visited July 26, 2020).
4. What we do, The National Urban League, https://nul.org (last visited May 28, 2020).
5. About Western Center, Western Center of Law & Poverty, WCLP.ORG, https://wclp.org/about-wclp/ (last visited July 26,

2020).
6. Dove: The Crown Research Study, static1.squarespace.com https://static1.squarespace.com/static/5ed-c69fd622c36173f56651f/t/5edeaa2fe5d-def345e087361/1591650865168/Dove_research_brochure2020_FINAL3.pdf (last visited July 26, 2020).
7. About, The Crown Act, THECROWNACT.COM, https://www.thecrownact.com/about (last visited July 26, 2020).
8. Danielle Meadows, Gov. Ricketts vetoes hair discrimination bill, 3NEWSNOW.COM, https://www.3newsnow.com/news/local-news/gov-ricketts-vetoes-hair-discrimination-bill (Posted at 5:44 PM, Aug 15, 2020 and last updated 6:27 PM, Aug 15, 2020).
9. Christina Santi, Black News Anchor Fired After Wearing "Unprofessional Natural Hair, EBONY (Jan. 16, 2019), https://www.ebony.com/culture/black-news-anchor-fired-unprofessional-natural-hair/.
10. News Anchor Symone Woolridge Called "Unprofessional" And Childish For Wearing Braids On Air, EMILYCOTTONTOP.COM, https://emilycottontop.com/news-anchor-symone-woolridge-called-unprofessional-and-childish-for-wearing-braids-on-air/ (last visited Aug. 15, 2020).Definition of braid, WWW.MERRIAN-WEBSTER.COM, https://www.merriam-webster.com/dictionary/braids (last visited Feb. 23, 2017).
11. What Are Dreadlocks?, HOWTOGETDREADS.COM, http://howtogetdreads.com/dreadlock-tutorials/preparing-for-dreadlocks/what-are-dreadlocks/ (last visited Feb. 23, 2017).
12. What Relaxers Really Do To Your Hair, BLACKDOCTOR.ORG, http://blackdoctor.org/216545/what-relaxers-really-do-to-your-hair__trashed/2/ (last visited Feb. 20, 2017).
13. Weaves vs Extensions, BLACK HAIR MEDIA, http://blackhairmedia.com/weave-and-extension/weaves-vs-extensions-2/ (last visited Feb. 23, 2017).
14. Definition of Afro, MERRIAM-WEBSTER.COM, https://www.merriam-webster.com/dictionary/Afro (last visited Mar. 2, 2017)
15. Enell B Stewart, 7 Cute Summer Puff Styles for Short, Medium

and Long Natural Hair, WWW.KINKYCURLYCOILYME.COM (July 11, 2014 at 9:32 am), https://www.kinkycurlycoilyme.com/7-cute-summer-puff-styles-for-short-medium-and-long-natural-hair/.

16. Rumeana Jahangir, How does black hair reflect black history?, May, 31, 2015, www.bbc.com; http://www.bbc.com/news/uk-england-merseyside-31438273.

17. Lee Moran, Ohio man, 20, claims dreadlocks cost him summer job at amusement park, May 11, 2015, www.nydailynews.com, http://www.nydailynews.com/news/national/ohio-man-20-claims-dreadlocks-cost-summer-job-article-1.2217641.

18. Susanna Kim, Ohio Man Claims Employer Told Him to Cut His Dreadlocks or Lose Job, May 8, 2015, ABCNEWS.GO.COM, http://abcnews.go.com/Business/ohio-man-claims-employer-told-cut-dreadlocks-lose/story?i Alex Janin, What the Perception of 'Professional' Hair Means for Black Job Seekers, Takepart.com, Apr. 13, 2016, http://www.takepart.com/article/2016/04/13/what-perception-professional-hair-means-black-job-seekers.d=30906401.

19. How To Create The Perfect Two-Strand Twist Out, WWW.ESSENCE.COM, http://www.essence.com/2016/07/11/perfect-two-strand-twist-out-how-to (last visited Feb. 23, 2017).

20. Maryline Dossou, Natural Hair vs. Corporate America: Why Are We Still Fighting This Battle?, EBONY.COM, July 3, 2013, http://www.ebony.com/style/fighting-for-our-hair-in-corporate-america-032#axzz4Q5o3casI.

21. Wig, DICTIONARY.COM, http://www.dictionary.com/browse/wig (last visited May 4, 2017).

22. Sabrina R Perkins, Natural Hair In The Workplace: What Are Your Rights? May Be A Viable Resource To Black Women, Essence.com, Jul 29, 2016, http://www.essence.com/2016/07/29/natural-hair-workplace-what-are-your-rights-may-be-viable-resource-black-women.

23. United States Department of Labor, Labor Force Characteristics by Race and Ethnicity, 2015, BUREAU OF LABOR STATISTICS (Sept. 2016) https://www.bls.gov/opub/reports/race-and-ethnicity/2015/home.htm.

24. Cornrow, WWW.DICTIONARY.COM, http://www.dictionary.com/browse/cornrow (last visited Feb. 23, 2017).
25. Hot Comb, WWW.MERRIAM-WEBSTER.COM, https://www.merriam-webster.com/dictionary/hot%20comb (last visited Feb. 23, 2017).
26. Biography: Madam C.J. Walker, WWW.BIOGRAPHY.COM, http://www.biography.com/people/madam-cj-walker-9522174 (last visited Apr. 13, 2017)
27. Henry Louis Gates, Jr., Madam Walker, The First Black American Woman to Be a Self-Made Millionaire, www.pbs.org, http://www.pbs.org/wnet/african-americans-many-rivers-to-cross/history/100-amazing-facts/madam-walker-the-first-black-american-woman-to-be-a-self-made-millionaire/ (last visited Feb. 22, 2017).
28. Antonia Opiah, The Changing Business of Black Hair, a Potentially $500b Industry, WWW.HUFFINGTONPOST.COM (Jan. 24, 2014), http://www.huffingtonpost.com/antonia-opiah/the-changing-business-of-_b_4650819.html.
29. Shelby Edwards, Relaxer Hair Sales Continue Decline as Black Hair Industry Aimed to Be Worth Over $774 Million, ATLANTABLACKSTAR.COM (July 29, 2015), http://atlantablackstar.com/2015/07/29/relaxer-hair-sales-continue-decline-as-black-hair-industry-aimed-to-be-worth-over-774-million/.
30. Chinwe, The Natural Hair Movement in the '60s and '70s; How It Began and Why It Ended, BLACKGIRLLONGHAIR.COM, Jan. 15, 2016, http://blackgirllonghair.com/2015/01/the-natural-hair-movement-in-the-60s-and-70s-how-it-began-and-why-it-ended.
31. The Fashion Bomb Staff, Black History Beauty Trend: The Jheri Curl, FASHIONBOMBDAILY.COM (Feb. 2, 2010), http://fashionbombdaily.com/black-history-beauty-trend-the-jheri-curl/.
32. U.S. Equal Employment
Opportunity Commission, About EEOC, https://www.eeoc.gov/eeoc/ (last visited Feb. 6, 2017).
33. U.S. Equal Employment Opportunity Commission, Prohibited Employment Policies/Practices: Dress Code, https://www.eeoc.gov/laws/practices/index.cfm (last visited Feb. 6,

2016).
34. Finger waves, www.merrian-webster.com, https://www.merriam-webster.com/dictionary/finger%20wave (last visited May 4, 2017).
35. Skully- a hat. SKULLYHAT.COM, http://skullyhat.com (last visited May 4, 2017).
36. Transatlantic Slave Trade, United Nations Educational, Scientific and Cultural Organization, http://www.unesco.org/new/en/social-and-human-sciences/themes/slave-route/transatlantic-slave-trade/ (last visited February 14, 2017).
37. Phenotype and Genotype, BIOMED.BROWN.EDU, https://biomed.brown.edu/Courses/BIO48/5.Geno.Pheno.HTML (last visited Apr. 8, 2017).
38. The Stanford at the Tech Understanding Technology: Other Traits, The Tech Museum of Innovation, genetics.thetech.org, April, 25, 2005, http://genetics.thetech.org/ask/ask107.
39. What Is Natural Hair?, BLACKHAIR.ABOUT.COM, http://blackhair.about.com/od/glossary/g/natural.htm (Last Updated May 06, 2016).
40. Ethnic differences in hair fiber and hair follicles, WWW.KERATIN.COM, http://www.keratin.com/aa/aa002.shtml (last visited Feb. 17, 2017).
41. Hair Straightening: The Hidden Dangers, FEELGOODSTYLE.COM, http://feelgoodstyle.com/2011/03/17/hair-straightening/ (last visited Feb. 17, 2017).
42. Chime Edwards, Real Talk About Heat Damage (Sept. 29, 2015), WWW.ESSENCE.COM, http://www.essence.com/2015/09/29/real-talk-about-heat-damage.
43. The beauty trend can cause headaches, baldness, and allergic reactions, CONSUMERREPORTS.ORG (Feb. 2013), http://www.consumerreports.org/cro/2013/02/the-dangers-of-hair-extensions/index.htm.
44. Pamela Vanderwerf, Synthetic Vs. Human Hair Extensions, WWW.LIVESTRONG.COM (Aug. 24, 2015), http://www.livestrong.com/article/66031-synthetic-vs.-human-hair-extensions/.

45. Janice Jackson, Understand the Dangers of Using Synthetic Hair Before You Buy It (June 25, 2012), http://worldhairextensions.com/blog/general/understand-the-dangers-of-using-synthetic-hair-before-you-buy-it.
46. ." Lauren A. Wise, Julie R. Palmer, David Reich, Yvette C. Cozier and Lynn Rosenberg, Hair Relaxer Use and Risk of Uterine Leiomyomata in African-American Women, Mar. 1, 2012, https://www.ncbi.nlm.nih.gov/pmc/articles/PMC3282879.
47. H. Fields Grenee, What Spending A Half A Trillion Dollars on Hair Care and Weaves Says About Us, madamenoire.com (May 11, 2011), http://madamenoire.com/57134/what-spending-a-half-a-trillion-dollars-on-hair-care-and-weaves-says-about-us/.
48. Black Voices, Black Women Avoiding Exercise To Maintain Hairstyles: Study, WWW.HUFFINGTONPOST.COM (Feb. 17, 2013), http://www.huffingtonpost.com/2012/12/18/black-women-hair-avoid-exercise_n_2321539.html.
49. Dr. Susan Taylor, Skin Care Tips for Men With Brown Skin, BROWNSKIN.NET (2008), http://www.brownskin.net/men.html.
50. Code of the District of Columbia, § 2–1401.02. Definitions, https://beta.code.dccouncil.us/dc/council/code/sections/2-1401.02.html (last visited Feb. 21, 2017).

Interview

1. Telephone interview Lindsay Thompson, Realtor, Keller Williams Town and Country (Feb. 6, 2017).
2. Interview with Andre L. Fletcher, Former Biology Laboratory Researcher, Texas Southern University Biology B.S., (Apr. 8, 2017).

Slogans

1. "Make America Great" idea taken from the 2016 Republican Candidate Donald Trump Campaign Slogan, Current President of The United States of America (2016).

My Hair Is Professional Too!

ABOUT THE AUTHOR

April Maria Williams, Esq.

April Maria Williams received her Juris Doctor from Florida A&M University College of Law and a Master's of Tax Law from the University of Houston. Since growing up in Elizabeth, New Jersey, April has always been an advocate for what is right. While studying for her undergraduate degree and master's degree at the University of Toledo, she began to see that her calling was that of a counselor. Not realizing at the time that she would be going into the legal field, she knew that her thoughts and opinions were valued because they spoke truth and were researched.

Williams is currently a licensed attorney practicing in Texas. She currently works as a Civil Attorney. April is passionate about promoting social justice and ensuring that everyone has a fair chance in today's society.

Made in United States
Orlando, FL
04 November 2026

90200510R00049